Egerton Castle, Agnes Castle

The Pride of Jennico

Being a Memoir of Captain Basil Jennico

Egerton Castle, Agnes Castle

The Pride of Jennico
Being a Memoir of Captain Basil Jennico

ISBN/EAN: 9783337078935

Printed in Europe, USA, Canada, Australia, Japan

Cover: Foto ©ninafisch / pixelio.de

More available books at **www.hansebooks.com**

THE PRIDE OF JENNICO

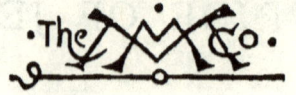

THE

PRIDE OF JENNICO

BEING

A Memoir of Captain Basil Jennico

BY

AGNES AND EGERTON CASTLE

New York
THE MACMILLAN COMPANY
LONDON: MACMILLAN & CO., LTD.
1898

Norwood Press
J. S. Cushing & Co. - Berwick & Smith
Norwood Mass. U.S.A.

THE PRIDE OF JENNICO

PART I

CHAPTER I

Memoir of Captain Basil Jennico (begun, apparently in great trouble and stress of mind, at the Castle of Tollendhal, in Moravia, on the third day of the great storm, late in the year 1771)

As the wind rattles the casements with impotent clutch, howls down the stair-turret with the voice of a despairing soul, creeps in long irregular waves between the tapestries and the granite walls of my chamber and wantons with the flames of logs and candles; knowing, as I do, that outside the snow is driven relentlessly by the gale, and that I can hope for no relief from the company of my wretched self,—for they who have learnt the temper of these wild mountain winds tell me the storm must last at least three days more in its fury,—I have bethought me, to keep from going melancholy crazed altogether, to set me some regular task to do.

And what can more fitly occupy my poor mind than the setting forth, as clearly as may be, the divers events that have brought me to this strange plight in this strange place? although, I fear me, it may not in the end be over-clear, for in sooth I cannot even yet see a way through the confusion of my thoughts. Nay, I could at times howl in unison with yonder dismal wind for mad regret; and at times again rage and hiss and break myself, like the fitful gale, against the walls of this desolate house for anger at my fate and my folly!

But since I can no more keep my thoughts from wandering to her and wondering upon her than I can keep my hot blood from running — running with such swiftness that here, alone in the wide vaulted room, with blasts from the four corners of the earth playing a very demon's dance around me, I am yet all of a fever heat — I will try whether, by laying bare to myself all I know of her and of myself, all I surmise and guess of the parts we acted towards each other in this business, I may not at least come to some understanding, some decision, concerning the manner in which, as a man, I should comport myself in my most singular position.

Having reached thus far in his writing, the scribe after shaking the golden dust of the pounce box over his page paused, musing for a moment, loosening with unconscious fingers the collar of his coat from his neck and gazing with wide grey eyes at the dancing flames of the logs, and the little clouds of ash that ever and anon burst from the hearth with a spirt when particles of driven snow found their way down the chimney. Presently the pen resumed its travels:

Everything began, of course, through my great-uncle Jennico's legacy. Do I regret it? I have sometimes cursed it. Nevertheless, although tossed between conflicting regrets and yearnings, I cannot in conscience wish it had not come to pass. Let me be frank. Bitter and troubling is my lot in the midst of my lonely splendour; but through the mist which seems in my memory to separate the old life from the new, those days of yesteryear (for all their carelessness and fancy-freedom) seem now strangely dull. Yes, it is almost a year already that it came, this legacy, by which a young Englishman, serving in his Royal and Imperial Majesty's Chevau-Legers, was suddenly transformed, from an obscure Rittmeister with little more worldly goods than his pay, into one of the richest landowners in the broad Empire, the master of an historic castle on the Bohemian Marches.

It was indeed an odd turn of fortune's wheel. But doubtless there is a predestination in such things, unknown to man.

My great-uncle had always taken a peculiar interest in me. Some fifty years before my birth, precluded by the religion of our family from any hope of advancement in the army of our own country, he had himself entered the Imperial service; and when I had reached the age of manhood, he insisted on my being sent to him in Vienna to enter upon the same career. To him I owe my rapid promotion after the Turkish campaign of 1769. But I question, for all his influence at Court, whether I should have benefited otherwise than through his advice and interest, had it not been for an unforeseen series of moves on the part of my elder brother at home.

One fine day it was announced to us that this latter had been offered and had accepted a barony in the peerage of Great Britain. At first it did not transpire upon what grounds a Catholic gentleman should be so honoured, and we were obliged, my uncle and I, to content ourselves with the impossible explanation that "Dear Edmund's value and abilities and the great services he had rendered by his exertions in the last Suffolk Elections had been brought to the notice of his Majesty, who was thus graciously pleased to show his appreciation of the same."

Our good mother (who would not be the true woman she is did she not set a value on the honours of this world), my excellent brother, and, of course, his ambitious lady, all agreed that it was a mighty fine thing for Sir Edmund Jennico to become My Lord Rainswick, and they sent us many grandiloquent missives to that effect.

But with my great-uncle things were vastly different. To all appearance he had grown, during the course of his sixty odd years in the Imperial service, into a complete unmitigated foreigner, who spoke English like a German, if, indeed, the extraordinary jargon he used (under the impression that it was his mother tongue) could be so called. As a matter of fact it would have been difficult to say what tongue was my great-uncle's own. It was not English nor French — not even the French of German courts — nor true German, but the oddest compound of all three, with a strong peppering of Slovack or Hungarian according as the country in which he served suggested the adjunction. A very persuasive compound it proved, however, when he took up his commanding voice, poor man! But, foreigner as he was, covered as his broad chest might be with foreign orders, freely as he had spent his life's energy in the pay of a foreign monarch, my great-uncle Jennico had too much English pride of race, too much of the old Jennico blood (despite this same had been so often let for him by Bavarian and Hanoverian, Prussian, French, and Turk), to brook in peace what he considered a slight upon his grand family traditions.

Now this was precisely what my brother had committed. In the first place he had married a lady who, I hear, is amazingly handsome, and sufficiently wealthy, but about whose lineage it seems altogether unadvisable to seek clear information. Busy as he was in the midst of his last campaign, my great-uncle (who even in the wilds of Bulgaria seemed to keep by some marvellous means in touch with what moves were being played by the family in distant Suffolk) nevertheless had the matter probed. And the account he received was not of a satisfactory nature. I fear me that those around him then did not find the fierceness of his rule softened by the unwelcome news from that distant island of Britain.

The Jennicos, although they had been degraded

(so my uncle maintained) by the gift of a paltry baronetcy at the hands of Charles II., as a reward for their bleeding and losses in the Royal cause, were, he declared, of a stock with which blood-royal itself might be allied without derogation. The one great solace of his active life was a recapitulation of the deeds, real or legendary, that, since the landing of the Danes on Saxon soil, had marked the passage through history of those thirty-one authentic generations, the twenty-ninth of which was so worthily represented by himself. The worship of the name was with him an absolute craze.

It is undoubtedly to that craze that I owe my accession of fortune — ay, and my present desolation of heart. . . .

But to resume. When, therefore, already dissatisfied with my brother's alliance, he heard that the head of the family proposed to engraft upon it a different name — a *soi-disant* superior title — his wrath was loud and deep:

"Eh quoi! mille millions de Donnerblitzen! what the Teufel idiot think? what you think?"

I was present when the news arrived; it was in his chancellerie on the Josefsplatz at Vienna. I shall not lightly forget the old man's saffron face.

"Does that Schaffkopf brother of yours not verstand what Jennico to be means? what thinkest thou? would I be what I am, were it not that I have ever known, boy, what I was geborn to when I was Jennico geborn? How comes it that I am what I here am? How is it gecome, thinkest thou, that I have myself risen to the highest honour in the Empire, that I am field-marshal this day, above the heads of your princekins, your grand-dukeleins, highnesses, and serenities? Dummes Vieh!"—with a parenthetical shake of his fist at the open paper on his desk—"how is it gecome that I wedded la belle Héritière des Woschutzski, the most beautiful woman in Silesia, the richest, pardi! the noblest?" And his Excellency (methinks I see him now) turned to me with sudden solemnity: "You will answer me," he said in an altered voice, "you will answer me (because you are a fool youth), that I have become great general because I am the bravest soldier, the cleverest commander, of all the Imperial troops; that I to myself have won the lady for whom Transparencies had sued in vain because of being the most beautiful man in the whole Kaiserlich service."

Here the younger Jennico, for all the vexation of spirit which had suggested the labour of his systematic narrative as a distraction, could not help smiling to himself, as, with pen raised towards the standish, he paused for a moment to recall on how many occasions he had heard this explanation of the Field-Marshal's success in life. Then the grating of the quill began afresh:

When my venerable relative came to this, I, being an irreverent young dog, had much ado to keep myself from a great yell of laughter. He was pleased to remark, latterly, in an approving mood, that I was growing every day into a more living image of what he remembered himself to have been in the good times when he wore a cornet's uniform. I should therefore have felt delicately flattered, but the fact is that the tough old soldier, if in the divers accidents of war he had gathered much glory, had not come off without a fine assortment of disfiguring wounds. The ball that passed through his cheeks at Leuthen had removed all his most ornamental teeth, and had given the oddest set to the lower part of his countenance. It was after Kolin that, the sight of his left eye being suppressed by the butt end of a lance, he had started that black patch which imparted a peculiar ferocity to his aspect, although it seemed, it is true, to sharpen the piercing qualities of the remaining orb. At Hochkirch, where he culled some of his greenest laurels, a Prussian bullet in his knee forced on him the companionship of a stout staff for ever afterwards. He certainly had been known in former days as *le beau Jennico*, but of its original cast of feature it is easy to conceive that, after these repeated finishing touches, his countenance bore but little trace.

"But no," the dear old man would say, baring his desolate lower tusks at me, and fixing me with his wild-boar eye, "it is not to my beauty, Kerl, not to my courage, Kerl, that I owe success, but because I am geborn Jennico. When man Jennico geborn is, man is geborn to all the rest — to the beauty, to the bravery. When I wooed your late dead tante, they, mere ignorant Poles, said to me: 'It is well. You are honoured. We know you honourable; but are you born? To wed a Countess Woschutzski one must be born, one must show, honoured sir,' they said, 'at least seize quartiers, attested in due proper form.'

"'Eh!' said I, 'is that all? See you, you shall have sixteen quarterings. Sixteen quarterings? Bah! You shall have sixteen quarterings beyond that, and then sixteen again; and you shall then learn what it is called to be called Jennico!' — Potztausend! — And I simply wrote to the Office of Heralds in London, what man calls College of Arms, for them to look up the records of Jennico and draw out a right proper pedigree of the familie, spare no cost, right up to the date of King Knut! Eh? Oh, ei, ei! Kerlchen! You should have seen the roll of parchment that was in time gesendt — *Teremtété!* and *les yeux que fit monsieur mon beau-père* [my excellent great-uncle said *mon peau-bère*] when they were geopened to what it means to be well-born English! A well-born man never knows his blood as he should, until he sets himself to trace it through all the veins. Blood-royal, yunker, blood-royal! Once Danish, two times Plantagenet, and once Stuart, but that a strong dose — he-he, ei, ei! The Merry Monarch, as the school-books say, had wide paternity, though — verstehts sich — his daughter (who my grossmutter became) was noble also by her mother. Up it goes high, weit. Thou shalt see for thyself when thou comest to Tollendhal. Na, ya, and thou shalt study it too — it all runs in thine veins also. Forget it not! . . . And of all her treasures, your aunt would always tell me there was none she prized more than that document relating to our family. She had it unrolled upon her bed when she could no longer use her limbs, and she used to trace out, crying now and then, the poor soul, what her boy would have carried of honour if he had lived. Ah, 'twas a million pities she never bore me another! — 'tis the only reproach that darf be made her. . . . I have consoled myself hitherto with the thought of my nephew's youthling; but, Potzblitz, this Edmund, now the head of our family — ach, the verdamned hound! Tausend Donnern and Bomben!" — and my great-uncle's guttural voice would come rumbling, like gathering thunder indeed, and rise to a frightful bellow — "to barter his fine old name for the verdamned mummery of a Baron Rainswick — Rainswick? — pooh! A creation of this Hanover dog! And what does he give on his side to drive this fine bargain? Na, na, sprech to me not: I mislike it; nephew, I tell thee, I doubt me but there is something hinter it yet.

"Nephew Basil," he then went on, this day I speak of, "if I were not seventy-three years old I would marry again — I would, to have an heir, by Heaven! that the true race might not die out!"

And despite his wall-eye, his jaw, his game leg, his generally disastrous aspect, I believe he might have been as good as his threat, his seventy-and-three years notwithstanding. But what really deterred him from such a rash step was his belief (although he would not gratify me by saying so) that there was at hand as good a Jennico as he could wish for, and that one, myself, Basil. And he saw in me a purer sproutling of that noble island race of the north that he was so fiercely proud of, than he could have produced by a marriage with a foreigner. For, thorough "Imperial" as he now was, and notwithstanding his early foreign education (which had begun in the Stuart regiments of the French king), the dominant thought in the old warrior's brain was that a very law of nature required the gentle-born sons of such a country to be honoured as leaders among foreign men. And great was the array of names he could summon, should any one be rash enough to challenge the assertion. Butlers and Lallys, Brownes and Jerninghams, by Gad! Keiths and Dillons and Berwicks, *morbleu!* Fermors, Loudons, and Lacys, and how many more if necessary; ay, and Jennicos not the least of them, I should hope, *teremtété!*

I did not think that my brother had bettered himself by the change, and still less could I concur in the turn-coat policy he had thought fit to adopt in order to buy from a Hanoverian King and a bigoted House of Lords this accession of honour. For my uncle was not far wrong in his suspicions, and in truth it did not require any strong perspicacity to realise that it was not for nothing my brother was thus distinguished. I mean not for his merits — which amounts to the same thing. I made strong efforts to keep the tidings of his cowardly defection from my uncle. But family matters were not, as I have said, to be hidden from Feldmarschall Edmund von Jennico. I believe the news hastened his dissolution. Repeated fits of anger are pernicious to gouty veterans of explosive temper. It was barely three weeks after the arrival of the tidings of my brother having taken the oaths and his seat in the House of Lords that I was summoned by a messenger, hot foot, from the little frontier town where I was quartered with my squadron, to attend my great-uncle's death-bed. It was a sixteen-hours' ride through the snow. I reached this frowning old stronghouse late at night, hastened by a reminder at each relay ready prepared for me; hastened by the servants stationed at the gate; hastened on the stairs, at his very door, the door of this room. I found him sitting in his armchair, almost a corpse already, fully conscious, grimly triumphant.

"Thou shalt have it all," was the first thing he whispered to me as I knelt by his side. His voice was so low that I had to bend my ear to his mouth.

But the pride of race had never seemed to burn with brighter flame. "Alles ist dein, alles . . . aber," and he caught at me with his clawlike hand, cold already with the very chill of earth, "remember that thou the last Jennico bist. Royal blood, Kerlchen, Knut, Plantagenet, Stuart . . . noblesse oblige, remember. Bring no roturière into the family."

His heiduck, who had endured his testy temper and his rigid rule for forty years, suddenly gave a kind of gulp, like a sob, from behind the chair where he stood, rigid, on duty at his proper post, but with his hands, instead of resting correctly on hip and sword-handle, joined in silent prayer. A striking-looking man, for all his short stature, with his extraordinary breadth of shoulders, his small piercing eyes, his fantastically hard features all pock-seared, that seemed carved out of some swarthy, worm-eaten old oak.

"Thou fool!" hissed my uncle, impatiently turning his head at the sound, and making a vain attempt to seek the ever-present staff with his trembling fingers. "Basil, crack me the knave on the skull." Then he paused a moment, looked at the clock and said in a significant way, "It is time, János."

The heiduck instantly moved and left the room,

to return promptly, ushering in a number of the retainers who had evidently been gathered together and kept in attendance against my arrival.

They ranged themselves silently in a row behind János; and the dying man in a feeble voice and with the shadow of a gesture towards me, but holding them all the while under his piercing look, said two or three times:

"Your master, men, your master." Whereupon, János leading the way, every man of them, household-steward, huntsmen, overseers, foresters, hussars, came forward, kissed my hand, and retired in silence.

Then the end came rapidly. He wandered in his speech and was back in the past with dead and gone comrades. At the very last he rallied once more, fixed me with his poor eye that I had never seen dim before, and spoke with consciousness:

"Thou, the last Jennico, remember. Be true. Tell the renegade I rejoice, his shame striketh not us. Tell him that he did well to change his name. Kerlchen, dear son, thou art young and strong, breed a fine stock. No roture! but sell and settle . . . sell and settle."

Those words came upon his last sigh. His eye flashed once, and then the light was extinguished.

Thus he passed. His dying thought was for the worthy continuance of his race. I found myself the possessor, so the tabellions informed me some days later, of many millions (reckoned by the florins of this land) besides the great property of Tollendhal — fertile plains as well as wild forests, and of this same isolated frowning castle with its fathom-thick walls, its odd pictures of half-savage dead and gone Woschutzskis, its antique clumsy furniture, tapestries, trophies of chase and war; master, moreover, of endless tribes of dependants: heiducks and foresters; females of all ages, whose bare feet in summer patter oddly on the floors like the tread of animals, whose high-boots in winter clatter perpetually on the stone flags of stairs and corridors; serf-peasants, factors, overseers; the strangest mixture of races that can be imagined: Slovacks, Bohemians, Poles, to labour on the glebe; Saxons or Austrians to rule over them and cypher out rosters and returns; Magyars, who condescend to manage my horseflesh and watch over my safety if nothing else; the travelling bands of gipsies, ever changing but never failing with the dance, the song and the music, which is as indispensable as salt to the life of that motley population.

And I, who in a more rational order of things

might have been leading the life of a young squire at home, became sovereign lord of all, wielding feudal power over strings of vassals who deemed it great honour to bend the knee before me and kiss my hand.

No doubt, in the beginning, it was vastly fine; especially as so much wealth meant freedom. For my first act, on my return after the expiration of my furlough, was to give up the duties of regimental life, irksome and monotonous in these piping days of peace. Then I must hie me to Vienna, and there, for the first time of my life of six-and-twenty years, taste the joy of independence. In Vienna are enough of dashing sparks and beautiful women, of princes and courtiers, gamblers and rakes, to teach me how to spend some of my new-found wealth in a manner suitable to so fashionable a person as myself.

But how astonishingly soon one accustoms oneself to luxury and authority! It is but three months ago that, having drained the brimming cup of pleasure to the dregs, I found its first sweetness cloying, its first alluring sparkle almost insufferable; that, having basked in perpetual smiles, I came to weary of so much favour. Winning at play had no fascination for a man with some thirty thousand pounds a year at his back;

and losing large slices of that patrimony which had, I felt, been left me under an implied trust, was dully galling to my conscience. I was so uniformly fortunate also in the many duels in which I was involved among the less favoured — through the kindness which the fair ladies of Vienna and Bude began to show to *le beau Jennico* (the old dictum had been revived in my favour) — that after disabling four of my newly-found "best friends," even so piquant an entertainment lost all pretence of excitement.

And with the progress of disillusion concerning the pleasure of idleness in wealth, grew more pressing the still small voice which murmured at my ear that it was not for such an end, not for the gratification of a mere libertine, gambler, and duellist, that my great-uncle Jennico had selected me as the depositary of his wealth and position.

"Sell and settle, sell and settle." The old man's words had long enough been forgotten. It was high time to begin mastering the intricacies of that vast estate, if ever I was to turn it to the profit of that stream of noble Jennicos to come. And in my state of satiety the very remoteness of my new property, its savageness, its proud isolation, invested it with an odd fascination. From one day to the other I determined on departure, and left the emptiness of the crowd to seek the fulness of this wild and beautiful country.

Here for a time I tasted interest in life again; knew a sort of well-filled peace; felt my soul expand with renewed vigour, keenness for work and deeds, hope and healthy desire, self-pride and satisfaction. Then came the foolish adventure which has left me naked and weak in the very midst of my wealth and power; which has left rudderless an existence that had set sail so gaily for glorious happiness.

The bell of the horologe, from its snow-capped turret overlooking the gate of honour in the stronghold of Tollendhal, slowly tolled the tenth hour of that tempestuous night; and the notes resounded in the room, now strongly vibrating, now faint and distant, as the wind paused for a second, or bore them away upon its dishevelled wing. Upon the last stroke, as Basil Jennico was running over the last page of his fair paper, the door behind him, creaking on its hinges, was thrown open by János, the heiduck, displaying in the next chamber a wide table, lit by two six-branched chandeliers and laid for the evening meal. The twelve yellow tongues of flame glinted on the silver, the cut glass, and the snow-white napery, but only to emphasise the sombre depth of the mediæval room, the desolate eloquence of that solitary seat at the huge board. János waited till his master, with weary gesture, had cast his pen aside, and then ceremoniously announced that his lordship's supper was ready.

Impatiently enough did the young man dip his fingers in the aiguière of perfumed water that a damsel on his right offered to him as he passed through the great doors, drying them on the cloth handed by another on his left. Frowning he sat him down in his high-backed chair behind which the heiduck stood ready to present each dish as it was brought up by other menials, to keep the beaker constantly filled, to answer with a bow any observation that he might make, should the lord feel disposed to break silence.

But to-night the Lord of Tollendhal was less disposed than ever in such a direction. He chafed at the long ceremony; resented the presence of these creatures who had seen her sit as their mistress at that table, where now lay nought but vacancy beyond the white cloth; resented even the silent solicitude that lurked in János's eyes, though the latter never broke unauthorised his rule of silence.

The generous wine, in the stillness and the

black solitude, bred presently a yet deeper melancholy. After a perfunctory meal the young man waved aside a last glass of the amber Tokay that was placed at his hand, rose, and moodily walked to and fro for some time. Feeling that the coming hours had no sleep in reserve for a mind in such turmoil as his, he returned to his writing-table, and, whilst János directed the servants to bring in and trim fresh candles, and pile more logs upon the hearth, Basil Jennico resumed his task.

CHAPTER II

BASIL JENNICO'S MEMOIR CONTINUED

My great-uncle's will, forcible, concise, indisputable as it was, had been (so the man of law informed me) drawn out in a great hurry, dictated, indeed, between spasms of agony and rage. (The poor old man died of gout in his stomach.) Doubtless, had he felt sure of more time, he would have burdened the inheritance with many directions and conditions.

From his broken utterances, however, and from what I had known of him in life, I gathered a fair idea of what his wishes were. His fifty years of foreign service had filled him, old pandour that he seemed to have become, with but increased contempt for the people that surrounded him, their ways and customs, while his pride as an Englishman was only equalled by his pride as a Jennico.

"Sell and settle . . ."

The meaning of the words was clear in the light of the man as I knew him. I was to sell the great property, carry to England the vast hoard of foreign wealth, marry as befitted one of the race, and raise a new and splendid line of Jennicos, to the utter mortification, and everlasting confusion, of the degenerate head of the house.

Now, though I knew it to be in me, and felt it, indeed, not otherwise possible, to live my life as true a Jennico as even my uncle could desire, I by no means deemed it incumbent upon me to set to work and carry out his plans without first employing my liberty and wealth as the humour prompted me. Nor was the old country an overpoweringly attractive place for a young man of my creed and kidney. In Vienna I was, perhaps, for the moment, the most noted figure — the guest most sought after that year. In England, at daggers drawn with my brother, I could only play an everyday part in an unpopular social minority.

It was in full summer weather that, as I have written, already tried by the first stage of my career of wealth, I came to take possession of my landed estates. The beauty and wildness of the scenery, the strangeness of the life in the well-nigh princely position to which this sudden turn of fortune's wheel had elevated me, the intoxicating sensation of holding sway, as feudal lord of these wide tracts of hill and plain, over so many hundreds of lives — above all, the wholesome reaction brought about by solitude and communion with nature after the turmoil of the last months — in short, everything around me and in me made me less inclined than ever to begin ridding myself of so fair a possession.

And do I wish I had not thus delayed in obeying the injunction that accompanied the bequest? Odds my life! I am a miserable dog this day through my disobedience; and yet, would I now undo the past if I could? A thousand times no! I hate my folly, but hug it, ever closer, ever dearer. The bitter savour of that incomprehensible yearning clings to the place: I would not exchange it for the tameness of peace. Weakling that I am, I would not obliterate, if I could, the memory of those brief, brief days of which I failed to know the price, until the perversity of fate cut their thread for ever — ay, perhaps for ever, after all! And yet, if so, it were wiser to quit these haunted walls for ever also. But, God! how meagre and livid looks wisdom, the ghost, by the side of love's warm and living line!

And now, on! Since I have put my hand to the task, undertaken to set forth and make clear the actual condition of that vacillating puppet, the new-fledged Lord of Tollendhal, I will not draw it back, cost me what pain it may.

No doubt it was this haunting pride of wealth, waxing every day stronger, even as the pride of birth which my great-uncle had fostered to such good purpose, the overweening conceit which they bred within me, that fogged my better judgment and brought me to this pass. And no doubt, likewise, it is a princely estate that these lords of Tollendhal of old carved for themselves, and rounded ever wider and nurtured — all that it should some day, passing through the distaff, come to swell the pride of Suffolk Jennicos!

My castle rises boldly on the northernmost spur of the Glatzer Mounts, and defiantly overlooks the marches of three kingdoms. Its lands and dependencies, though chiefly Moravian, extend over the Bohemian border as well as into that Silesia they now are able to call Prussian. North and west it is flanked by woods that grow wilder, denser, as they spread inwards towards the Giant Mountains. On the southern slopes are my vineyards, growths of note, as I hear. My territories reach, on the one hand, farther than can be seen under the blue horizon, into the Eastern plains, flat and rich, that stretch with curious suddenness immediately at the foot of the high district; upon the other hand, on the Moravian side, I doubt whether even my head steward himself knows exactly how much of the timber-laden hill-ranges can be claimed as appertaining to the estate. All the peaks I can descry in a fine day from these casements are mine, I believe; on their flanks are forests as rich in game — boar and buck, wolf and bear, not to speak of lesser quarry — as are the plains below in corn and maize and cattle — *que sais-je?* A goodly heritage indeed!

I promised myself many a rare day's sport so soon as the time waxed ripe. Meanwhile, my days were spent in rambles over the land, under pretence of making acquaintance with the farms and the villages, and the population living on the soil and working out its wealth for my use, but in reality for the enjoyment of delicious sylvan and rustic idleness through which the memory of recent Viennese dissipations was like that of a fevered dream.

The spirit of my country-keeping ancestors lived again within me and was satisfied. Yet there were times, too, when this freedom of fancy became loneliness — when my eyes tired of green trees, and my ears hungered for the voice of some human being whom I could meet as an equal, with whom I could consort, soul and wit. Then I would resolve that, come the autumn, I would fill the frowning stronghouse with a rousing throng of gallant hunters and fair women such as it had never seen before. Ay, and they should come over, even from old England, to taste of the Jennico hospitality!

It was in one of these glorious moods that, upon a September day, sultry as summer, although there was a touch of autumn decay in the air as well as in the tints around me, I sallied forth, after noon, to tramp on foot an as yet unexplored quarter of my domain. I had donned, according to my wont (as being more suitable to the roughness of the paths than the smallclothes, skirted coats, high heels and cocked hat of Viennese fashion), the dress of the Moravian peasant —I gather that it pleases the people's heart to see their seigneur grace their national garb on occasions. There was a goodly store of such costumes among the cupboards full of hereditary habiliments and furs preserved at Tollendhal, after the fashion of the country, with the care that English housewives bestow upon their stores of linen. My peasant suit was, of course, fine of cloth and natty of cut, and the symmetry of the handsome figure I saw in my glass reminded me more of the pastoral disguises that were the courtly fashion of some years back than of our half-savage ill-smelling boors. Thus it was pleasant as well as comfortable to wear, and at that time even so trifling a sensation of gratified vanity had its price. But, although thus freed of the incumbrance of a gentleman's attire, I could not shake off the watchful tyranny of János, the solemn heiduck who never allowed me to stir abroad at all without his escort, nor, indeed (if my whim took me far afield), without the further retinue of two jägers, twin brothers, and faithful beyond a doubt. These, carbine on shoulder, and hanger on thigh, had their orders to follow their lord through thick and thin, and keep within sight and sound of whistle.

In such odd style of state, on this day, destined to begin for me a new chapter in life, I took my course; and for a long hour or so walked along the rocky cornice that overhangs the plains. The land looked bare and wide and solitary, the fields lay in sallow leanness bereft of waving crops, but I knew that all my golden grain was stacked safely in the heart of the earth, where these folk hoard its fruits for safety from fire. The air was so empty of human sounds, save the monotonous tramp of my escort behind me, that all the murmurs of wind and foliage struck with singular loudness upon my ear. Over night, there had, by my leave, been songs and dancing in the courtyard of Tollendhal, and the odd tunes, the capricious rhythm of the gipsy musicians, came back upon me as I walked in the midst of my thoughts. These melodies are fitful and plaintive as the sounds of nature itself, they come hurrying and slackening, rising and falling, with as true a harmony and as unmeasured a measure, — now in a very passion of haste, and now with a dreamy long-drawn sigh. I was thinking on this, and on the love of the Empress for that music (my Empress that had been when I wore her uniform, ay, and my Empress still so long as I retain these noble lands), when I came to a field, sloping from the crag towards the plain, where an aftermath of grass had been left to dry. There was a little belt of trees, which threw a grateful shade; and feeling something weary I flung me down on the scented hay. It was on the Silesian portion of my land. Against the horizon, the white and brown of some townlet, clustering round the ace-of-club-shaped roof of its church-tower, rose glittering above the blue haze. A little beyond the field ran a white road. So I reclined, looking vaguely into the unknown but inviting distance, musing on the extent of those possessions so widespread that I had not as yet been able to ride all their marches, ever and anon recognising vaguely in the voice of the breeze through the foliage an echo of the music that had been haunting my thoughts all day. Everything conspired to bring me pleasant fancies. I began to dream of past scenes and future fortunes, smiling at the thought of what my dashing friends would say if they saw *le beau Jennico* in this bucolic attitude, wondering if any of my Court acquaintances would recognise him in his peasant garb.

Ah me, how eternally and lovingly I thought of my proud and brilliant self then! . . .

I cannot recall how soon this musing became deep sleep, but sleep I did and dream—a singular, vivid dream, which was in a manner a continuation of my waking thoughts. I seemed to be at a great *fête* at the Imperial Palace, one of the countless throng of guests. The lights were brilliant, blinding, but I saw many faces I knew, and we all were waiting most eagerly for some wonderful event. No one was speaking, and the only sounds were the rustling and brushing of the ladies' brocades and the jingle of the officers' spurs, with over and above the wail of the czimbalom. All at once I knew, as we do in dreams, what we were expecting, and why this splendid feast had been prepared. Marie Antoinette, the fair young Dauphine of France, the memory of whose grace still hangs about the Court, had come back to visit her own country. The crowd grew closer and closer. The crowd about me surged forward to catch a glimpse of her as she passed, and I with the rest, when suddenly my great-uncle stood before me, immensely bestarred and beribboned in his field-marshal's uniform, and with the black patch on his eye so black that it quite dazzled me.

"Na, Kerlchen," he was saying to me, "thou hast luck! Her Imperial and Royal Highness has chosen the young Jennico to dance with . . . as the old one is too old."

Now I, in common with the young men about me, have grown to cherish since my coming to this land a strange enthusiasm for the most womanly and beautiful of all the Empress's daughters, and therefore, even in my dream, my heart began to beat very fast, and I scarce knew which way to turn. I was much troubled too by the music, which went on always louder and quicker above my head, somewhere in the air, for I knew that no such things as country dances are danced at Court, and that I myself would make but a poor figure in such; yet a peasant dance it undoubtedly was. Next, my uncle was gone, and though I could not see her, I knew the Princess was coming by the swish of her skirt as she walked. I heard her voice as clear as a silver bell. "*Où est-il?*" it said, and I felt she was looking for me. I struggled in vain to answer or turn to her, and the voice cried again: "*Où est-il?*" upon which another voice with a quaver in its tones made reply: "*Par ici, Altesse!*"

The sound must have been very close to me, for it startled me from my deep sleep into, as it were, an outer court of dreams. And between slumber and consciousness I became aware that I was lying somewhere very hot and comfortable; that, while some irresistible power kept my eyes closed, my ears were not so, and I could hear the two voices talking together; and, in my wandering brain believed them still to belong to the Princess Marie Antoinette and her attendant.

"It is a peasant," said the first voice: that was the Princess of course. There was something of scorn in the tone, and I became acutely and unpleasantly conscious of my red embroidered shirt. But the other made answer: "He is handsome," and then: "His hands are not those of a peasant," and, "*Regardez ma chère;* peasants do not wear such jewelled watches!" A sudden shadow fell over me and was gone in an instant. There was a flicker of laughter and I sat up.

During my sleep the shade of the sun had

shifted and I lay in the full glare, and so, as I opened my eyes, I could see nothing.

I heard the laughter of my dream again, and I knew that the mocking cry of "*Prenez garde, Altesse!*" that still rang in the air did not belong to my sleep. But as I rubbed my eyes and looked out once again, I caught first a glimpse of a slender creature bending over me, outlined it seemed in fire and shimmering between black and gold. My next glance filled me with a woeful disappointment, for I declare, what with my dream and my odd awakening, I expected to find before me a beauty no less bewitching than that of her Royal Highness herself. What I beheld was but a slim slip of a creature who, from the tip of her somewhat battered shepherdess hat to the hem of her loosely hanging skirts, gave me an impression of being all yellow, save for the dark cloud of her hair. Her skin seemed golden yellow like old ivory, her eyes seemed to shoot yellow sparks, her gown was yellow as any primrose. As she bent to watch me, her lip was arched into a smile; it had a deep dimple on the left side. Thus I saw her in a sort of flash and scrambled to my feet still half drunk with drowsiness, crying out like a fool:

"*Où est son Altesse? Où est son Altesse?*"

She clapped her hands and turned with a crow of laughter to some one behind me. And then I became aware that, as in the dream, there were two. I also turned.

My eyes were in their normal state again, but for a moment I thought myself still wandering. Here was her Highness. A Princess, indeed, as beautiful as any vision and yet most exquisitely embodied in the flesh; a Princess in this wilderness! It seemed a thing impossible, and yet my eyes now only corroborated the evidence of my ears.

I marked, almost without knowing, the rope of pearls that bound her throat (I had become a judge of jewels by being the possessor of so many). I marked her garments, garments, for all their intended simplicity, rich, and bearing to my not untutored observation the latest stamp of fashion. But above all I marked her air of race, her countenance, young with the first bloom of youth, mantled with blushes yet set with a royal dignity.

I have, since that eventful day, passed through so many phases of feeling, sweet and violent, my present sentiments are so fantastically disturbed, that I must try to the last of this writing and see matters still as I saw them at the time. Yes, beyond doubt what I noticed most, what appealed to me most deeply then, was the great air of race blended and softened by womanly candour and grace. She looked at me gravely, with wide brown eyes, and I stumbled into my best courtly bow.

"He wants to know," said the damsel of the yellow skirts, this time in German, the clear, clean utterance of which had nothing of the broad Austrian sounds I was accustomed to hear — "he wants to know 'where is the Highness?' But he seems to have guessed where she stands, without the telling. Truly 'tis a pity the Lord Chamberlain is not at his post to make a presentation in due form!"

The lady thus addressed took a step towards her companion, with what seemed a protest on her lip. But the latter, her small face quivering with mischief and eagerness, whispered something in her ear, and the beautiful brown eyes fixed themselves once again smilingly on me.

"Know, sir," continued the speaker then, "since you are so indiscreet as to wake at the wrong moment, and surprise an incognito, the mysteries of which were certainly not meant for such as you, that Altesse she is. *Son Altesse Sérénissime la Princesse Marie Ottilie.* Marie is her Highness's first name, and Ottilie is her Highness's last name. And between the two and after those two, being as I said an Altesse Sérénissime, she has of course a dozen other names; but more than this it does not suit her Highness that you should know. Now if you will do me, a humble attendant that I am, the courtesy to state who you are, who, in a Silesian boor's attire, speak French and wear diamond watches to your belt, I can proceed with the introduction, even in the absence of the Lord Chamberlain."

The minx had an easy assurance of manner which could only have been bred at Court. Her mistress listened to her with what seemed a tolerant affection.

Looking round, bewildered and awkwardly conscious of my peasant dress, I beheld my two chasseurs, standing stolidly sentinel on the exact spot where I had last seen them before dropping asleep. Old János, from a nearer distance, watched us suspiciously. As I thus looked round I became aware of a new feature in the landscape — a ponderous coach also attended by two chasseurs in unknown uniforms waiting some hundred paces off, down the road.

To keep myself something in countenance despite my incongruous garb (and also perchance for the little meanness that I was not displeased to show this Princess that I too kept a state of my own), I lifted my hand and beckoned to my retinue, which instantly advanced and halted in a rank with rigid precision five paces behind me.

"Gracious madam," said I in German, bowing to her who had dubbed herself the lady-in-waiting, with a touch, I flattered myself, of her own light mockery of tone, "I shall indeed feel honoured if her Serene Highness will deign to permit the presentation of so unimportant a person as myself — in other words of Basil Jennico of Farringdon Dane, in the county of Suffolk, in the Kingdom of Great Britain, lately a captain in his Royal Imperial Majesty's Moravian Regiment of Chevau-Legers, now master of the Castle of Tollendhal, not far distant, and lord of its domain." Here, led by János, my three retainers saluted.

I thought I saw in the Princess's eyes that I had created a certain impression, but my consequent complacency did not escape the notice of the irrepressible lady-in-waiting. She promptly did her best to mar the situation.

"Fi donc," she cried, in French, "we are at Court, Monsieur, and at the Court of — at the Court of her Highness we are not such savages as to perform introductions in German."

Then, drawing up her slight figure and composing her face into preternatural gravity, she took two steps forward and another sideways, accompanied by as many bows, and resting her hand at arm's length on the china head of her stick, with the most ridiculous assumption of finikin importance and with a quavering voice which, although I have never known him, I recognised instantly as the Chamberlain's, she announced:

"Monsieur Basile Jean Nigaud de la Faridondaine, dans le comté où l'on Suffoque, . . . d'importance, au royaume de la Grande Bretagne, maître du Castel des Fous, ici proche, et seigneur des alentours, — ahem!"

Inwardly cursing the young woman's buffoonery and the incredible facility with which she had so instantly burlesqued an undoubtedly impressive recital, I had no choice but to make my three bows with what good grace I could muster. Whereupon, the Princess, still smiling but with a somewhat puzzled air, made me a curtsey. As for the lady-in-waiting, nothing abashed, she took an imaginary pinch of most excellent snuff with a pretence of high satisfaction; then laughed aloud and long, till my ears burned and her own dimple literally rioted.

"And now, to complete the ceremony," said she, as soon as she could speak at all, "let me introduce the Court, represented to-day by myself. Mademoiselle Marie Ottilie. Two Ottilies as you will perceive, but easily explained, thus: Feu the Highest her Sérénissime's gracious ducal grandmother being an Ottilie and godmother to us both —Mademoiselle Ottilie: the rest concerns you not. Well, Monsieur de la Faridondaine, Capitaine et Seigneur, etc., etc., — charmed to have made your acquaintance. So far, so good. But . . . these gentlemen? Surely also nobles in disguise. Will you not continue the ceremony?"

She waved a little sunburnt hand towards my immovable body-guard, and the full absurdity of my position struck me with the keenest sense of mortification.

I looked back at the three, biting my lips, and miserably uncertain how to conduct myself so as to save some shred of dignity. My ancient János had seen too many strange things during his forty years' attendance on my great-uncle to betray the smallest surprise at the present singular situation; but out of both their handsome faces, set like bronze, — they had better not have moved a muscle otherwise or János would have known the reason why, — the eyes of my twin attendants roamed from me to the ladies, and from the ladies to me, with the most devouring curiosity. I tartly dismissed them all again to a distance, and then, turning to the mysterious Princess I begged to know, in my most courtlike manner if I might presume to lay my services at her feet for the time of her sojourn in this, my land.

With the same adorable yet dignified bashfulness that I had already noted in her, the lovely woman looked hesitatingly at her lady-in-waiting, which lively wench, not being troubled with timidity (as she had already sufficiently demonstrated), promptly took upon herself to answer me. But this time she so delightfully fell in with my own wishes that I was fain to forgive her all that had gone before.

"But certainly," she exclaimed, "her Serene Highness will condescend to accept the services of M. de Jean Nigaud. It is not every day that brings forth such romantic encounters. Know, sir, that we are two damozels that have by the most extraordinary succession of fortunate accidents escaped from school. You wonder? By school, I mean the insupportable tedium, etiquette, and dulness of the Court of his most gracious and worshipful Serenity the father of her Highness. We came out this noon to make hay, and hay we will make. Or rather we shall sit on the hay, and you shall make a throne for the Princess, and a little tabouret for me, and then you may sit you down and entertain us . . . but on the ground, and at a respectful distance, that none may say we do not observe proper forms and conventions, for all that we are holiday-making. And you shall explain to us how you, an Englishman, came to be master of Château des Fous, and masquerading in peasant's attire. Is masquerading a condition of tenure? After which, her Serene Highness having only one fault, that being her angelic softness of heart, which is pushed to the degree of absolute weakness, she will permit me to narrate to you (as much as is good for you to know) how we came to be here at such a distance from our own country, and in such curious freedom — for her Highness quite sees that you are rapidly becoming ill with suppressed curiosity, and fears that you may otherwise burst with it on your way home to your great castle, or at least that the pressure on the brain may seriously affect its delicate balance — if indeed," with a peal of her reckless childish laughter, "you are not already a lunatic, and those your keepers!"

This last piece of impudence might have proved even too much for my desire to cultivate an acquaintance so extraordinarily attractive to one of my turn of mind and so alluring by its mysteriousness, but that I happened to catch a glance from her Highness's eyes even as the speaker finished her tirade, which glance, deprecating and at the same time full of a kindly and gentle interest, set my heart to beat in a curious fashion between pleasure and pain. I hastened therefore to obey the younger lady's behests, and began to gather together enough of the sweet-smelling hay to form a throne for so noble and fair an occupant.

Whereupon the little creature herself — she seemed little by reason of her slenderness and childishness, but in truth she was as tall as her tall and beautiful mistress — fell to helping me with such right goodwill, flashing upon me, as she flitted hither and thither, such altogether innocently mocking looks from her yellow-hazel eyes, that I should have been born with a deeper vanity, and a sourer temper, to have kept a grudge against her.

Once seated in our fragrant court, in the order laid down for us, the attendant, so soon as she had recovered breath sufficient, began to ply me with questions so multiplied, so searching, and so pointed, that she very soon extracted from me every detail she wished to know about myself, past and present.

But although, as from a chartered and privileged advocate, the sharp cross-questioning came from the Mademoiselle Marie Ottilie, it was to the soft dumb inquiry I read in the Princess Marie Ottilie's eyes that were addressed my answers. And then those eyes and the listening beauty of that gracious face, made it hard for me to realise, as later reflection proved, that their owner did not utter a single word during the whole time we sat there together.

CHAPTER III

I MIND me that when she had drawn from me all she had wanted to know, the little lady's pert tongue became still for a while, and that she stretched her long young limbs and lay back upon her mound of hay with the most absolute unconcern either of my presence or of the Princess's, gazing skyward with a sudden gravity in her look. As for me, I was content to sit in silence too, glad of the quiet, because it gave me leisure to taste the full zest of this fortunate and singular meeting. I thought I had never seen a human being whom silence became so well as the Princess Ottilie. Contrasted with the recklessness and chatter of her companion her attitude struck me as the most perfectly dignified it had ever been my lot to observe.

Presently the nymph in yellow roused herself from her reverie, and sat up, with her battered hat completely on one side and broken bits of grass sticking in the tangled mass of her brown hair. She arched her lip at me with her malicious smile, and addressed her companion.

"Is it your Highness's pleasure," she asked, "that I should gratify some of this young English nobleman's curiosity concerning the wandering of a Princess in so unprincely a fashion?"

"Ach!" rebuked her Highness, on the wings of a soft sigh. The truth of the girl's assertion that her mistress's kindness of heart amounted to weakness, was very patent; the dependant was undoubtedly indulged to the verge of impertinence, although it is also true that her manner seemed to stop short of any open show of disrespect.

"Now attention, please, Monsieur de la Faridondaine! His Most Absolutely to be Revered and Most Gracious Serenity, father of her Highness, reigns over a certain land, a great many leagues from here," she began, with all the gusto of one who revels in the sound of her own voice. "Her Highness is his only daughter, and this August Person has the condescension to feel for her some of those sentiments of paternal affection which are common even to the lowest peasant. You have been about Courts, Monsieur Jean Nigaud, the fact is patent and indubitable. You can therefore realise the extent of such condescension. A little while ago, moved by these sentiments, my gracious Sovereign believed there was a paleness upon her Highness his daughter's cheek."

Involuntarily I looked at the Princess, to see, with a curious elation, how the rich colour rushed, under my gaze, yet more richly into her face.

"It does not appear now," pursued the imperturbable speaker, whom no blink of mine seemed to escape, "but there *was* a paleness, and the Court doctor decided there was likewise a trifling loss of tone and want of strength. He recommended a change of air, tonic baths, and grape cure. In consequence, after due deliberation and consultation, it was decreed that her Highness should be sent to a certain region in the mountains, where Höchst die Selbe has a grand, a most high, ducal aunt, the said region being noted for its salubrious air, its baths, the quality and extent of its vineyards. In company, therefore, of a few indispensable court officials — the Lord Chamberlain (as a responsible person for her Highness's movements), the most gracious a certain aged and high born Gräfin (our chief Court lady, once the Highness's own gouvernante), the second Court doctor, the third officier de bouche, and mine own humble self ——"

Here she paused, and, with a sudden assumption of dolefulness that was certainly comic, proceeded in quite another voice:

"I am a person of no consequence at Court,

Monsieur de la Faridondaine. I am merely tolerated because of her Highness's goodness, and also because, you must know, that I have a reputation of being a source of amusement to her Serenity. You may already have noticed that it is fairly well founded that I am talkative and entertaining, as a lady-in-waiting should be, and this is the reason why I have attained a position to which my birth does not entitle me."

A little frown came across the Princess's smooth brow at these words. She shot a look of deprecation at her attendant, but the latter went on, resuming her former manner, in a bubbling of merriment:

"Facts are facts, you see — I am even hardly *born*. My mother happened to be liked by the mother of her Serene Highness — an angel — and when I was orphaned she took me closer to her. So we grew up together, her Highness and I, and so I come to be in so grand a place as a Court. There, Monsieur, you have in a word the history of Mademoiselle Marie Ottilie. I have no wish that she should ever seem to have appeared under false colours."

The Princess, whose sensitive blood had again risen to a crimson tide, cast a very uneasy look at her companion. I could see how much her affectionate delicacy was wounded by this unnecessary candour.

But little mademoiselle, after returning the glance with one as mischievous and unfeeling as a jackdaw's, continued, hugging her knees with every appearance of enjoyment:

"And now we come to the series of delightful accidents which brought us here. Behold! no sooner had we left the Court of — the Court her Highness belongs to — than the smallpox broke out in the Residenz and in the palace itself. The father of her Serenity had had it; there was no danger for *him*, and he was in the act of congratulating himself upon having sent the Princess out of the way, when, in the most charming manner (for the Ducal Court of her Highness's aunt was even duller than Höchst die Selbe's own, and after the tenth bunch of grapes you get rather tired of a grape cure, and as for mud baths — oh fie, the horror!), we discovered that we had brought the pretty illness with us. And first one and then the other of the retinue sickened and fell ill. Then a Court lady of the Duchess took it, and next who should develop symptoms but the old growl-bear and scratch-cat, our own chief Hofdame, chief duenna, and chief bore. That was a stroke of fortune, you must admit! But wait a moment, you have not heard the best of it yet."

At the very first mention of the smallpox the Princess grew pale, and made the sign of the cross. And indeed it seemed to me, myself, a tempting of Providence to joke thus lightly about a malady so dangerous to life and so fatal to looks. But the girl proceeded coolly:

"Her Serene Highness, like her most venerated brother, had had the disease; I believe they underwent it together in their Serene Babyhood. But her Serene Highness was deeply alarmed by the danger to which her Serene niece was exposed. The Court doctor was no less concerned —it is a bad thing for a Court doctor if a princess in his charge fall a victim to an epidemic — so they put their heads together and resolved to send the exalted young lady into some safer region, in company of such of her retinue as seemed in the soundest health. An aged lady, mother of M. de Schreckendorf, our Chamberlain already described to you, dwells in these plains. As a matter of fact," said the speaker, pointing a small finger in the direction of the town, "her castle is yonder. The Duchess had once condescended to spend a night there to break a journey, and it had remained stamped on her ducal memory that the place was quiet,—not to say a desert,—that there were vineyards close by, and also that the air was particularly salubrious. She knew, too, that the Countess Schreckendorf was quite equal to the guarding of any youthful Serenity, in short, a dragon of etiquette, narrow-mindedness, prudery, and ugliness. Together, therefore, with the Chamberlain, a few women, and the poor doctor, we were packed into a ducal chariot, and carted here, the Countess receiving the strictest orders not to divulge the tremendous altitude of her visitor's rank. She would die rather than betray the trust, —especially as to thwart innocent impulses is one of her chief pleasures, nay, I may say her only pleasure in life. Little does she or the Highness her mistress suspect the existence of a Seigneur de la Faridondaine, roaming about in the guise of a simple Silesian shepherd and pretending to sleep in order to surprise the little secrets of wandering princesses! We were told, when we asked whether there was no neighbourly creature within reach, that the only one for leagues was a fearful old man with one eye and one tooth, who goes about using his cane as freely on every one's shoulders as the Prussian king himself. Well, never mind, don't speak, I have yet the cream of the tale to offer! We arrived here three weeks ago and found the grapes no more spicy, the castle no more amusing, and the neighbourhood more boring than even the ducal Court itself. But one excellent day, the good little Chamberlain began to look poorly, complained of his poor little head, and retired to his room. The next morning what does the doctor do, but pack *him* into a coach and drive away with him like a fury. Neither coach, nor postillions, nor doctor, nor Chamberlain, have been seen or heard of since! But I, who am awake with the birds, from my chamber window saw them go — for I heard the clatter in the courtyard, and by nature, M. the Captain, I am as curious as a magpie."

"Oh, that," said I with conviction, "you need not tell me!"

She seemed vastly tickled by the frankness of this my first observation after such long listening, and had to throw herself back on the hay, and laugh her laugh out, before she could sit up again and continue:

"So, as I was saying, I saw the departure. The doctor looked livid with fright, and as for the Herr Chamberlain, he was muffled up in blankets and coats, but I got a glimpse of his face for all that, and *it was spotted all over with great red spots!*"

The Princess pushed her hat off her forehead, and turned upon her lady-in-waiting a face that had grown almost livid.

"Pooh!" said the lady-in-waiting; "your Highness is over-nervous; 'tis now a good fortnight since the old gentleman left us, and if you or I were to have had it we should have shown symptoms long ago. Well, sir, to continue: our worthy hostess the Countess was in a fine fume, as you can fancy, between duty and natural affection, terror and anxiety. She was by way of keeping the whole matter a dead secret both from us and from the servants; but the fumigations she set going in the house, the airing, the dosing, together with her own frantic demeanour, would have been enough to enlighten even obtuser wits than ours. With one exception all our servants fled, and all hers. She had to replace them from a distance. The anger, the responsibility, the agitation generally, were too much for her years and constitution; and three days ago — in the act (as we discovered) of writing to the Duchess for instructions, for she had expected the Court doctor would have sent on special messengers to the courts of her Highness's relatives, and was in a perfect fever at receiving no news — as I say, in the very act of writing evidently to despatch another post herself, the poor old lady was struck with paralysis, and was carried speechless to bed. Now, Monsieur Jean Nigaud, you English are a practical race. Do you not agree with me that since the Lord, in His wisdom, decreed that it was good for the Countess's soul to have a little physical affliction, it could not have happened at a better moment for us? I know that her Highness disapproves of what she calls my heartlessness, but I cannot but rejoice in our freedom.

"The Countess is recovering, but she won't speak plain for a long time to come. Meanwhile we are free — free as air! Our only personal attendant is my own — my old nurse. You shall see her. She speaks but little, but she adores me. But as we cannot understand a word of the language spoken here, and the resources of this district are few, I will own to you, her Highness has found it a little dull, in spite of her lady-in-waiting's well-known gift of entertainment, up to to-day."

She threw me an arch look as she spoke, but the Princess, rising with the dignity peculiar to her, conveyed her sense that the joke had this time been carried a little too far.

The shadows were lengthening, the wind had fallen, it was an hour of great peace and beauty in the land. The Princess took a few steps towards the road where waited the carriage; I ran forward and presumed to offer her my arm, which she very graciously, but not without a blush, accepted. The maid of honour, springing to her feet, followed us, tripping over the rough ground, with a torn frock and her hat hanging on her neck by its ribbons. I mind me well how the chasseurs of the equipage stared to see their lady come leaning on the arm of a peasant. How they stared, too, at the unabashed, untidy apparition of the lady-in-waiting! But she, humming a little song as she went, seemed the last in the world to care what impression she made.

As we neared the coach, a tall woman all in black, with a black shawl over her black hair, jet-black eyes, staring blankly out of a swarthy face, descended from it. She looked altogether so dark and forbidding a vision that I gave a start when I saw her thus unexpectedly. She seemed a sort of blot on the whole smiling, sunny landscape. But as Mademoiselle Ottilie drew near, the woman turned to her, her whole face breaking pleasantly into a very eloquence of silent, eager love.

Of course I guessed at once that this was the nurse to whom the saucy maiden had already referred. I heard them whisper to each other (and it seemed to me as if the woman were remonstrating with her mistress) while I installed the Princess on her cushions. Then both rejoined us to enter the carriage likewise. Before she jumped in, Mademoiselle Ottilie tapped her nurse on the shoulder with the sort of indifferent, kind little pat one would bestow on a dog. The woman caught the careless hand and kissed it, and her eyes as she looked after the girl's figure were absolutely adoring; but her whole countenance again clouded over strangely when her glance fell upon us. At length they all three were seated, and my graceful retirement was clearly expected. But still I lingered.

"The vintage had begun in my vineyards," quoth I hesitatingly; "if her Highness would honour me by coming again upon my lands, the sight might interest her."

The Princess hesitated, and then, evidently doubtful as to the propriety of the step, threw a questioning glance at her companion.

"But certainly," said the latter instantly, "why not accept? Your Highness has been advised to keep in the open air as much as possible, and your Highness has likewise been recommended innocent diversion: nothing could be better. When shall we say?"

"If to-morrow would suit," I suggested boldly, "I could ride over after noon, if her Highness would permit me to be her escort. And perhaps she will also further honour me by accepting some slight refreshment at my castle. It is worth seeing," I said, for I saw no reason why I should be bashful in pushing my advantages, "if your Highness is not afraid to enter Le Château des Fous?" I ventured to look deep into her eyes as I spoke, and I remember how those eyes wavered shyly from my gaze, and how the white lids fell over them. And I remember, too, with what a sudden mad exultation leaped my heart.

But, as before, it was the lady-in-waiting who answered.

"Afraid! who is afraid? Your Highness, will you not comfort the poor young man and tell him you are not afraid?"

"If your Highness would deign," said I, pleadingly, and leaning forward into the carriage.

And then she looked at me, and said to me in the sweetest guttural in all the world, "No, I am not afraid."

We were speaking French. I bowed low, fearing to spoil it all by another word. The Princess stretched out her hand and I kissed the back of her glove, and then I had the privilege of also kissing Miss Ottilie's sunburnt, scratched, and rather grimy bare little paw, which she, with affected dignity, thrust forward for my salute.

The carriage drove away, and as it went I mind me how the nurse looked after me with a darkling anxiety, and also how as I stalked homewards through the evening glow, with my body-guard tramping steadily behind me, I kept recalling the sound of the four gracious words with which the Princess had consented to accept of my hospitality.

She had said, it is true, "*Che n'ai bas beur,*" but none the less was the memory a delicate delight to my heart the whole night through.

CHAPTER IV

I HAD questioned János on our homeward way concerning my new acquaintances; but the fellow was so ill-disposed by nature to external gossip, so wholly occupied with the minute fulfilment of his daily task, which was to watch over the well-being and safety of his master, that he had gathered no acquaintance with affairs outside his province. With the head factor, however, whom I sent for immediately after supper, I was more fortunate. This man, Karl Schultz, is Saxon-born, and consequently one of the few of my numerous dependants with whom I can hold converse here. It was but natural that among the peasantry the advent of strangers, evidently of wealth and distinction, should have created some stir, and it is Schultz's business, among many other things, to know what the peasantry talk about; although in this more contented part of the world this sort of knowledge is not of such importance as among our neighbours the Poles. Schultz, therefore, was aware of the arrival of the ladies, likewise of the rumour of smallpox, which had, so he informed me, not only driven all the servants out of the Castle of Schreckendorf, but spread something like a panic over the country-side. Tidings had also come to his ears that two gentlemen — one of them suffering from the dreadful malady (doubtless the poor Chamberlain) — had been abandoned in their carriage by their postillions and servants at the small village of Kittlitz, some forty miles from here, just over the Lusatian border. He corroborated, in fact, greatly to my joy, all that I had been told; for I had had an uneasy fear upon me, now and again, as I marched home in the evening chill, that I had been too ready to lend credence to a romantic and improbable story. But, better than all, Schultz, having felt a special curiosity concerning visitors from his own country, had, despite the attempt to keep the matter secret, contrived to satisfy himself to the full as to their identity. And thus did I, to my no small triumph, from the first day easily penetrate the ill-guarded incognita.

The beautiful wandering Princess was the only daughter of the old reigning house of Lausitz-Rothenburg; and it was from Georgenbrunn, where she had been on a visit to her aunt the Dowager Duchess of Saxony, that the second outbreak of the epidemic had driven her to take refuge with the Countess Schreckendorf in our neighbourhood.

Vastly satisfied with my discovery, and not a little fluttered by the impending honour, I made elaborate preparations the next day against the coming of such guests. We rifled the gardens, the greenhouses, and the storerooms, and contrived a collation the elegance of which taxed our resources to the uttermost.

Not in peasant garb did I start at noon upon my romantic quest, but in my finest riding suit of mulberry cloth embroidered with green and silver, (of what good auguries did I not think when I remembered that green and white were actually the colours of the Maison de Lusace, and that in this discreet manner I could wear on my sleeve the mark of a delicate homage?), ruffles of finest Mechlin fluttered on my throat and wrists, and a hat of the very latest cock was disposed jauntily at the exact angle prescribed by the Vienna mode.

With my trim fellows behind me, and with as perfect a piece of horseflesh between my knees as the Emperor himself could ever hope to bestride, I set out in high delight and anticipation.

Now, on this freezing winter's night, when I look back upon those days and the days that followed, it seems to me as though it were all a dream. The past events are wrapped to memory in a kind of haze, out of which certain hours marked above the rest stand out alone in clearness. — That particular day stands forth perhaps the clearest of all.

I remember that the Princess Ottilie looked even more queenly to my mind than at first, with her fair hair powdered and a patch upon the satin whiteness of her chin. In the complacency of my young man's vanity, I was exceedingly elated that she should have considered it worth while to adorn herself for me. I remember, too, that the lady-in-waiting examined me critically, and cast a look of approval upon my altered appearance; that she spoke less and that her mistress spoke more than upon our first meeting; that even the presence, mute, dark, and scowling, of their female attendant could not spoil the pleasure of our intercourse.

In the vineyards, it is true, an incident occurred which for a moment threatened to mar my perfect satisfaction. The peasant girls — it is the custom of the country on the appearance of strangers in the midst of their work — gathered round each lady, surrounding her in wild dancing bands, threatening in song to load her shoulders with a heavy hodful of grapes unless she paid a ransom. It was of course most unseemly, considering the quality of the company I was entertaining, and I had not foreseen the possibility of such a breach of respect. Never before, it was evident, in the delicately nurtured life of the Princess, had such rough amusement been allowed to approach her. This being the case, it was not astonishing that the admirable composure of her usual attitude should break down —her dignity give way to the emotion of fear. She called — nay, she screamed — to me for help. The while her pert lady-in-waiting, no whit abashed, laughed back at her circle of grinning sunburnt prancers, threw mocking good-humoured gibes at them in German, and finally was sharp enough to draw her purse and pay for her footing, crying out to her mistress to do the same. But the latter was in no state to listen to advice, and, alas! I found myself powerless to deliver the distressed lady. In my ignorance of their language I could do nothing short of use brute force to control my savages, who were after all (it seems) but acting in good faith upon an old-established privilege. So I was fain, in my turn, to summon Schultz to the rescue from a distant part of the ground. He, practical fellow, made no bones about the matter; with a bellow and a knowing whirl of his cane every stroke of which told with a dull thwack, he promptly dispersed the indiscreet merrymakers.

I suppose it is my English blood that rises within me at the sight of a woman struck. Upon the impulse of the first moment I had well-nigh wrenched the staff from his hands and laid it about his shoulders; but fortunately, on second thought, I had wisdom enough to refrain from an act which would have been so fatal to all future discipline. Nevertheless, as I stood by, a passive spectator of it, the blood mounted, for very shame, to my cheek, and I felt myself degraded to the level of my administrator's brutality.

The poor fools fell apart, screaming between laughter and pain. One handsome wench I marked, indeed, who withdrew to the side of a sullen gipsy-looking fellow, her husband or lover apparently; and as she muttered low in his ear they both cast looks charged with such murderous import, not only at the uncompromising justiciary, but also at me, and the man's hand stole instinctively to his back with so significant a gesture, that I realised for the first time quite fully that there might be good reasons for János's precautions anent the lord's precious person when the lord took his walks abroad.

Another girl passed me close by, sobbing aloud, as she returned to her labour. She rubbed her shoulder sorely, and the tears hopped off the rim of her fat cheeks, contorted like those of a blubbering child. In half-ashamed and sneaking fashion, yet unable to resist the urging of my heart, I followed her behind the next row of vines and touched her on the arm.

She recognised me with a start, and I, all fearful of being noticed by the others, in haste and without a word — as what word could I find in which to communicate with a Slovack? — hastily dropped a consolatory coin, the first that met my touch, into her palm.

It was a poor plain creature with dull eyes, coarse lips, and matted hair, and she gazed at me a moment stupidly bewildered. But the next instant, reading I know not what of sympathy and benevolence in my face, as a dog may read in his master's eyes, she fell at my feet, letting the gold slip out of her grasp that she might the better seize my hand in hers and cover it with kisses, pouring forth the while a litany of gratitude, as unintelligible to me as if she had been indeed a dog whining at my feet.

To put an end to the absurd situation, distasteful to my British free-born pride for all my foreign training, I pushed her from me and turned away, to find the lady-in-waiting at my elbow.

Instead, however, of making my weakness a mark for her wit, this latter, to my great relief, and likewise to my astonishment, looked wistfully from the ugly besmeared face to the coin lying on the black soil, then at my countenance, which at that moment was, I felt, that of a detected schoolboy. And then, without a word, she followed me back to her mistress's side.

My august visitor had not yet regained her wonted serenity. Still fluttered, she showed me something of a pouting visage. I thought to discern in her not only satisfaction at the punishment she had seen administered, but some resentment at my passive attitude. And this, I confess, surprised me in her, who seemed so gentle and womanly. But I told myself then that it was but natural in one born as she was to a throne.

On the other hand, while I confounded myself in excuses and explanations, blaming myself for having (through my inexperience of this country) neglected to prevent the possibility of so untoward an incident, I heard behind me the voice of the young Court lady, rating Schultz in most explicit German for the heaviness of his hand upon my folk. And, as the Princess gradually became mollified towards me and showed me once again her own smiling graciousness, I contrasted her little show of haughtiness with the unreserve of her companion, and convinced myself that it did but become her (being what she was). The while I watched Mademoiselle Ottilie, mingling with peasants as if she had been born among them, with an ever renewed wonder that she should have been chosen for the high position she occupied.

Later on my guest, according to her promise, condescended to rest and refresh herself in the castle. This was the culminating moment of a golden afternoon. I felt the full pride of possession when I led her in through the old halls that bore the mark of so many centuries of noble masters; although indeed, as a Jennico, I had no inherited right to peacock in the glories of the House of Tollendhal. But, at each portrait before which she was gracious enough to halt, I took care to speak of some notable contemporary among the men and women of my own old line, in that distant enchanted island of the North, where the men are so brave and strong and the women so fair. And, without stretching any point, I am sure the line of Jennico lost nothing in the comparison.

She was, I saw, beyond mistake impressed. I rejoiced to note that I was rapidly becoming a person of importance in her eyes. Even the lady-in-waiting continued to measure me with an altered and thoughtful look.

Between the eating of our meal together—

which, as I said, was quite a delicate little feast, and did honour to my barefooted kitchen retinue — and the departure of my visitors, I took them through many of the chambers, and showed them some of the treasures, quaint antiquities, and relics that my great-uncle had inherited or himself collected. On a little table under his picture — yonder on that wall it hangs before me — I had spread forth in a glass case, with a sort of tender and pious memory of the rigid old hero, his own personal decorations and honours, from the first cross he had won in comparative youth to the last blazing order that a royal hand had pinned over the shrunken chest of the field-marshal. In this portrait, painted some five years before his death, my uncle had insisted on appearing full face, with a fine scorn of any palliation of the black patch or the broken jaw. It is a grim enough presentment in consequence, — the artist having evidently rather relished his task, — and sometimes, indeed, when I am alone here in this great room at night, and it seems as if the candle-light does but serve to heighten the gloom of the shadows, I find my uncle's one eye following me with so living a sternness that I can scarce endure it.

But that day of which I am writing, I thought there was benignity in the fierce orb as it surveyed such honourable company, and even an actual touch of geniality in the set of the black patch.

As I opened the case, both the ladies fell, women-like, to fingering the rich jewels. There was a snuff-box set around with diamonds, upon the lid of which was painted a portrait of the Dauphine. This, Maria Theresa had herself given to my uncle on the occasion of her daughter's marriage, to which it was deemed my uncle's firm attitude in council over the Franco-Austrian difficulty had not a little contributed.

With a cry of admiration, the Princess took it up. "Ach, what diamonds!" she said. I looked from the exquisite face on the ivory to the no less exquisite countenance bending above it, and I was struck by the resemblance which had no doubt unconsciously been haunting me ever since I first met her. The arch of the dark eyebrow, the supercilious droop of the eyelid, the curve of the short upper lip, and the pout of the full under one, even the high poise of the head on the long throat, were curiously similar. I exclaimed upon the coincidence, while the Princess flushed with a sort of mingled pleasure and bashfulness.

Mademoiselle Ottilie took up the miniature in her turn, and, after gravely comparing it with her own elfish, sunburnt visage in the glass, gazed at her mistress; then, heaving a lugubrious sigh, she assented to my remarks, adding, however, that there was no ground for surprise, as the Princess Marie Ottilie was actually cousin to her Royal Highness the Dauphine.

The Princess blushed again, and lifted up her hand as if to warn her companion. But the latter, with her almost uncanny perspicacity, continued, turning to me:

"Of course, M. de Jennico" (she had at last mastered my name) — "of course, M. de Jennico has found out all about us by this time, and is perfectly aware of her Highness's identity."

Then she added, and her eyes danced:

"Since M. de Jennico is so fond of genealogy" (among the curiosities of the place I had naturally shown them my uncle's monumental pedigree), "he can amuse himself in tracing the connection and relationships — no doubt he has the 'Almanach de Gotha' — between the houses of Hapsburg and the Catholic house of Lausitz-Rothenburg."

And indeed, although she meant this in sarcasm, when, after I had escorted them home, I returned, through the mists and shades of twilight, to my solitude (now peopled for me with delightful present, and God knows what fantastic future, visions), I did produce that excellent new book, the "Almanach de Gotha," and found great interest in tracing the blood-relation between the Dauphine and the fairest of princesses. And afterwards, moved by some spirit of vainglory, I amused myself by comparing on the map the relative sizes of the Duchy of Lausitz and the lands of Tollendhal.

And next I was moved to unroll once again my uncle's pedigree, and to study the fine chain of noble links of which I stand the last worthy Jennico, when something that had been lying unformed in my mind during these last hours of strange excitement suddenly took audacious and definite shape.

CHAPTER V

WHAT first entered my brain as the wildest possibility grew rapidly to a desire which possessed my whole being with absolute passion. The situation was in itself so singular and tantalising, and the Princess was so beautiful a woman, to be on these terms of delicious intimacy with the daughter of one of Europe's sovereigns (a little sovereign it is true, but great by race and connection), to meet her constantly in absolute defiance of all the laws of etiquette, yet to see her wear through it all as unapproachable a dignity, as serene an aspect of condescension, as though she were presiding at her father's Court — it was enough, surely, to have turned the head of a wiser man than myself!

It was not long before Mademoiselle Ottilie, the lady-in-waiting, discovered the secret madness of my thoughts — in the light of what has since occurred I can truly call it so. And she it was who, for purposes of her own, shovelled coals on the fire and fanned the flame. One way or another, generally on her initiative, but always by her arrangement, we three met, and met daily.

On the evening of a day passed in their company, with the impression strong upon me of the Princess's farewell look, which had held, I fancied, something different to its wont; with the knowledge that I had, unrebuked, pressed and kissed that fair hand after a fashion more daring than respectful, with my blood in a fever and my brain in a whirl, now seeming sure of success, now coldly awake to my folly, I bethought me of taking counsel again with my great-uncle's pedigree. And heartened by the proofs that the blood of Jennico was good enough for any alliance, I fell to completing the document by bringing it up to date as far as concerned myself. Now, when I in goodly black letters had set down my own cognomen so fair upon the parchment, I was further seized with the fancy to fill in the space left blank for my future marriage; and I lightly traced in pencil, opposite the words "Basil Jennico, Lord of Tollendhal," the full titles and names, which by this time I had studied till I knew them off by heart, of her Serene Highness the Princess Marie Caroline Dorothée Josephine Charlotte Ottilie of Lausitz.

It made such a pretty show after all that had

gone before, and it brought such visions with it of the glories the name of Jennico might yet rise to, that I could not find it in me to erase it again, and so left it as it stood, telling myself, as I rolled up the great deed again and hooked it in its place beneath my uncle's portrait, that it would not be my fault if the glorious entry did not remain there for ever.

The next time the ladies visited me, Mademoiselle Ottilie — flitting like a little curious brown moth about the great room, dancing pirouettes beneath my uncle's portrait, and now and again pausing to make a comical grimace at his forbidding countenance, while I entertained her mistress at its further end — must needs be pricked by the desire to study the important document, which I had, as I have said, already submitted to her view.

Struck by her sudden silence and stillness, I rose and crossed the room to find her with the parchment rolled out before her, absorbed in contemplation, her elbows on the table, her face leaning on her hands. With a fierce rush of blood to my cheeks, in a confusion that set every pulse throbbing, I attempted to withdraw from her the evidence of what must seem the most impudent delusion. But she held tight with her elbows, and then, disregarding my muttered explanation that I intended to rub out at once the nonsense I had written in a moment of idleness, she laid her small finger upon the place, and, looking at me gravely, said:

"Why not?"

The whole room whirled round with me.

"My God," I cried, "don't mock me!"

But she, with a new ring of feeling in her voice, said earnestly:

"She has such misery before her if her father carries out his will."

To hear these words from her, who of all others must be in her mistress's confidence, ought, however amazing to reason and common sense, to have been a spur to one whose ambition soared so high. Nevertheless, I hesitated. To be honest with myself, not from a lover's diffidence, from a lover's dread of losing even hope, but rather from the fear of placing myself in an absurd position — of risking the deadly humiliation of a refusal.

I dared therefore nothing but soft looks, soft words, soft pressures of the hand; and the Princess received them all as she received everything that had gone before. From one in her position this might seem of itself encouragement enough in all conscience; but I waited in vain for some break in her unruffled composure — some instant in which I could mark that the Princess was lost in the woman. And so what drew me most to her kept me back. At the same time a rooted distrust of the little lady-in-waiting, a certain contempt, too, for her personality as belonging to that roture so despised of my great-uncle and myself, prevented me from placing confidence in her.

But she, nevertheless, precipitated the climax. It was three days after the scene in my great-uncle's room, one Sunday morning, beside the holy-water font in the little chapel of Schreckendorf Castle, whither, upon the invitation of its present visitors — my own priest being ill, poor man, of an ague — I had betaken myself to hear mass. The Princess had passed out first, and had condescended, smiling, to brush the pious drops from my finger; but Mademoiselle Ottilie paused as she too touched with hers my outstretched hand, and said in my ear as crossly as a spoilt child:

"You are not a very ardent lover, M. de Jennico. The days are going by; the Countess Schreckendorf is beginning to speak quite plain again. It is impossible that her Highness should be left in this liberty much longer."

I caught her hand as she would have hurried away.

"If I could be sure that this is not some foolish jest," I said in a fierce whisper in her ear.

And she to me back again as fiercely:

"You are afraid!" she said with a curling lip.

That settled it.

I rode straight home, though I was expected to have joined the ladies in some expedition. I spent the whole day in a most intolerable state of agitation; and then, my mind made up, I sat down after supper to write, beneath my uncle's portrait. And the first half of the night went by in writing and re-writing the letter which was to offer the hand and heart of Basil Jennico to the Princess Marie Ottilie of Lausitz.

I wrote and tore up till the ground around me was strewn with the fragments of paper; and now I seemed too bold, when the whole incongruity and absurdity of my desire took tangible form to mock me in the silence of the night; and now too humble, when in the flickering glimmer of candle-light my great-uncle would frown down upon me, and I could hear him say:

"Remember that thou Jennico bist!"

At last a letter lay before me by which I resolved to abide. I believe that it was an odd mixture of consciousness of my own temerity in aspiring so high, and at the same time of conviction that the house of Jennico could only confer, and not receive, honour. I even proposed to present myself boldly with my credentials at the Court of Lausitz (and here of course the famous pedigree came in once more), and I modestly added that, considering my wealth and connections, I ventured to hope the Duke, her father, might favourably consider my pretensions.

This written and sealed, I was able to sleep for the rest of the night, but was awake again with dawn and counting the minutes until I could decently despatch a mounted messenger to Schreckendorf.

When the man rode forth I believe it was a little after eight; and I know that it was on the stroke of one when I heard his horse's hoofs ringing again in the courtyard. But time had no measure for the strange agony of doubt in which I passed those hours, not (once again have I to admit it) because I loved her too dearly to bear the thought of life without her, but because of my fierce pride, which would not brook the shame of a refusal.

I called in a frenzy to hurry the lagging fool into

my presence; and yet when he laid the letter on my table I stared at the great seal without daring to open it. And when at last I did so my hand trembled like an aspen leaf.

"Monsieur de Jennico," it began abruptly, "I ought to call you mad, for what you propose is nothing less indeed than madness. You little know the fetters that bind such lives as mine, and I could laugh and weep together to think of what the Duke, my father, would say were you really to present yourself before him as you suggest."

So it ran, and as I read I thought I was contemned, and in my fury would have crushed the letter in my hand, when a word below caught my eye, and with an intensity of joy on a par only with the passion of wounded pride that had preceded it, I read on:

"But, dear Monsieur de Jennico," so ran the letter then, "since you love me, and since you honour me by telling me so; since you offer me so generously all you have to give, I will be honest with you and tell you that my present life has no charm for me. I know only too well what the future holds for me in my own home, and I am willing to trust myself to you and to your promises rather than face the lot already drawn for me .

"Therefore, Monsieur de Jennico, if it be true that, as you say, all your happiness depends upon my answer, I trust it may be for the benefit of both that I should say 'Yes' to you to-day. But what is to be must be secretly done, and soon.

Are you willing, to obtain your desire, to risk a little, when I am willing to risk so much in granting it? If so, meet my lady-in-waiting to-day at six, alone, where we first met, and she will tell you all that I have decided."

It was signed simply — "Marie Ottilie."

There was no hint of answering love to my passionate declaration, but I did not miss it. I had won my Princess, and the few clear words in which she laid bare before me the whole extent of my presumption only added to the exquisite zest of my conquest.

It was a very autumn day — autumn comes quickly in these lands. It had been raining, and I rode down from the higher level into a sea of white writhing mists. It was still and warm — one of those heavy days that as a rule seem like to clog the blood and fill one with reasonless foreboding. I remember all that now; but I know that there was no place for foreboding in my exulting heart as I sallied out full early to the trysting-place.

The mare I rode, because of the close atmosphere and her own headstrong temper, was in a great lather when I arrived at the little pine-wood, and I dismounted and began to lead her gently to and fro (for I loved the pretty creature, who was as fond and skittish as a woman) that she might cool by degrees and take no injury. I was petting and fondling her sleek coat, when of a sudden, without my having had the least warning of her coming, I turned to find Mademoiselle Ottilie before me.

She looked at me straight with one of those odd searching looks which I had now and again seen her fix upon me; and without either "Good-even" or "How-do-you-do," she said abruptly:

"I saw you coming all the way along the white road from the moment it turns the corner, and I saw how your mare fought you, and how difficult it was to bring her past the great beam of the well yonder. You made her obey, but you have not left a scratch upon her sides — yet you wear spurs."

She looked at me with the most earnest inquiry, and, ruffled by the futility of the question when so much was at stake, I said to her somewhat sharply:

"What has this to do, Mademoiselle, with our meeting here to-day?"

"It has this to do, Monsieur," she answered me composedly, "that her Highness's interests are as dear to me as my own, and that I am glad to learn that the man she is to wed has a merciful heart. I know a man," she went on, "in our own country who passes for the finest, the bravest, the most gallant, but when he brings a horse in from the

G

chase its legs will be trembling and it will be panting so that it can scarce draw breath, because the rider is so brave and dashing that he must go the fastest of all, and he will have left his mark upon the poor beast's sides in great furrows where he has ploughed them with his spurs. He is greatly admired by every one; but his horses die, and his hounds shrink when he moves his hand: that is what my country-people call being manly — being a real cavalier!"

The scorn of her tone was something beyond the mere girlish pettishness I generally associated with her; but to me, except as she represented or influenced her mistress, she had never had any interest. And so again impatiently I brought her back to the object of our meeting.

"Her Highness has entrusted you with a message?" I asked.

"Her Highness would first of all know," said the maid of honour, "if you fully realise the difficulties you may bring upon yourself by the marriage you propose?"

"'The Princess," said I proudly, "has condescended to say that she will trust herself to me. After that, as far as I am concerned, there can be no question of difficulty. As for her, if she will consent to accompany me to England, no trouble or reproach need ever reach her ears. If she prefers to remain here, I shall none the less be able to protect my wife, were it against the whole Empire itself."

"That is the right spirit," said Mademoiselle Ottilie, nodding her head approvingly. "What you say has not got a grain of common sense, but that is all as it should be. And next," she continued, drawing closer to me, for there was a twilight dimness about us, and standing on tiptoe in the endeavour to bring her gaze on a level with mine, "her Highness wishes to know" — she dropped her voice a little — "if you love her very much?"

As if the gaze of those yellow hazel eyes of hers had cast a sudden revealing light upon my soul, I stood abashed and dumb, self-convicted by my silence. Love! Did I love her whom I would make my wife? Taken up with schemes of vainglory and ambition, what room had I in my heart for love? In all my triumph at having won her, was there one qualifying thread of tenderness? Would I, in fine, have sought the woman, beautiful though she was, were she not the Princess?

In a sort of turmoil I asked myself these things under the compelling earnestness of Mademoiselle Ottilie's eyes, and everything in myself looked strange and hideous to myself, as beneath a vivid lightning flash the most familiar scene assumes a singular and appalling aspect.

In another moment she moved away and turned aside from me; and then, even as after the lightning flash all things resume their normal aspect, I wondered at my own weak folly, and my blood rose hotly against the impertinence that had evoked it.

"By what right," said I, "Mademoiselle, do you ask me such a question? If it be indeed by order of her Highness, pray tell her that when she will put it to me herself I will answer it to herself."

The maid of honour wheeled round with her arch, inscrutable smile.

"Oh!" she said, "believe me, you have answered me very well. I was already convinced of the sincerity and ardour of your attachment to ... her Highness — so convinced, indeed, that I am here to-night for the sole purpose of helping both you and her to your most insane of marriages. The Princess is accustomed to rely upon me for everything, and upon me, therefore, falls the whole burden of preparation and responsibility. Whether the end of all this will be a dungeon for the lady-in-waiting, if indeed the Duke does not have her executed for high treason, is naturally a

contingency which neither of you will consider
worth a moment's thought. It is quite certain,
however, that without me you would both do
something inconceivably stupid, and ruin all.
But, voyons, Monsieur de Jennico," she went on
with sudden gravity of demeanour, "this is no time
for pleasantry. It is a very serious matter. You
are wasting precious moments in a singularly
light-hearted fashion, it seems to me."

The reproach came well from her! But she
left me no time to protest.

"I am here," she said, "as you know, to tell
you what the Princess has decided, and how we
must act if the whole thing is not to fail. First
of all, the arrival of some important person from
the Court of Lausitz may take place any day, and
then — 'Bonjour!'" She blew an airy kiss and
waved her hand, while with a cold thrill I realised
the irrefutable truth of her words.

"If it is to be," she went on, unconsciously repeating almost the exact text of her mistress's
letter to me, "it must be at once and in secret.
Mind, not a word to a soul till all is accomplished!
On your honour I lay it! And she, her Highness,
enjoins it upon you not to betray her to any single
human being before you have acquired the right to
protect her. It is surely not too much to ask!"

She spoke with deep solemnity, and yet characteristically cut short my asseverations.

"And, that being settled, and you being willing to take this lady for your wife, — probably without a stiver, and certainly with her father's curse" (I smiled proudly in the arrogance of my heart: all Duke as he was I did not doubt, once the first storm over, but that my exalted father-in-law would find very extenuating circumstances for his wilful daughter's choice), — "that being settled," continued Miss Ottilie, "it only remains to know — are you prepared to enter the marriage state two nights hence?"

"I wish," said I, and could not keep the note of exultation from my voice at having the rare prize thus actually within my reach — "I wish you would ask me for some harder proof of my complete devotion to her Highness."

"Well, then," she said hastily, whispering as if the pines could overhear us, "so be it! I have not been idle to-day, and I have laid the plot. You know the little church in that wretched village of Wilhelmsdhal we posted through two days ago? The priest there is very old and very poor and like a child, because he has always lived among the peasants; and now indeed he is almost too old to be their priest any more. I saw him to-day, and told him that two who loved each other were in great straits because people wanted to wed the maiden to a bad and cruel man,— that is true, Monsieur de Jennico, — I told him that these two would die of grief, or lose their souls, perhaps, were they separated, because of the love they bore each other. . . . There, sir, I permitted myself a poetical license! To be brief, I promised him in your name what seemed a great sum for his poor, a thousand thalers — you will see to that — and he has promised me to wed you on Wednesday night, at eight of the clock, secretly, in his poor little church. He is so old and so simple it was like misleading a child, but nevertheless, the cause being good, I trust I may be forgiven. Drive straight to the church, and there you will find one who will direct you. The Princess will not see you again till she meets you before the altar. You will bring her home to your castle. A maid will accompany her. And that is all. Adieu, Monsieur de Jennico."

She stretched out her hand and her voice trembled.

"You will not see the maid of honour perhaps ever again. Her task is done," she added.

I took her hand, touched by her accent of earnestness, and gratefully awoke to the fact that she alone had made the impossible possible to my desire. I looked at her face, close to mine in the faint light; and as she smiled at me, a little sadly, I was struck with the delicate beauty of the curve of her lip, and the exquisite finishing touch of the dimple that came and went beside it, and the thought flashed into my mind — "That little maid may one day blossom into the sort of woman that drives men mad."

She slipped her hand from mine as I would have kissed it, and nodded at me with a return of the cool impudence that had so often vexed me.

"Good-bye, gallant cavalier," she said mockingly.

She whistled as if for a dog, and I saw the black figure of the nurse start from the shadow of the trees a few yards away, and, meeting, they joined in the mist and merged swiftly into it.

Whereupon I mounted the mare, who was sorely tried by her long waiting; and as we cantered homewards I was haunted, through the extraordinary blaze of my triumphant thoughts, to my own exasperation and surprise, oddly and unwillingly, by the arch sweetness of the maid of honour's smile.

And once (I blushed all alone in the darkness for the shame of such a thought in my mind at such a moment) I caught myself picturing the sweetness a man might find in pressing his lips upon the tantalising dimple.

CHAPTER VI

The night before my wedding-day — it was natural enough — there was a restlessness upon me which would not let me sleep, or think of sleep.

When supper was over I bade my servants retire. They had thought me cracked, and with reason, I believe, for the way in which I had wandered about the house all day, moving and shifting and preparing, and giving orders to no seeming purpose. I sat down in my uncle's room, and, drawing the chair he had died in opposite his portrait, I held a strange conclave with (as I believed then) his ghost. I know now that if any spirit communed with me that night it was my own evil angel.

I had had the light set where it best illuminated the well-known countenance. At my elbow was a goodly bottle of his famous red wine.

"Na, old one," said I aloud, leaning back in my chair in luxurious self-satisfaction and proud complacency, "am I doing well for the old name? Who knows if one day thou countest not kings among thy descendants!"

Methought the old man grinned back at me, his hideous tusked grin.

"'Tis well, Kerlchen," he said.

I unrolled the pedigree. That cursed parchment, what a part it has played in my life!—as evil a part, as fatal as the apple by which our first parents fell. It is pride that damns us all! And I read aloud the entries I had made: they sounded very well, and so my uncle thought—or seemed to—for I swear he winked at me and said:

"Write it in ink, lad; that must stand clear, for das klingt schön."

And then, though I was very comfortable, I had to get up and find the ink and engross the noble record of my marriage, filling in the date with care, for my uncle, dead or alive, was not one to disobey.

"'Tis good," then again said my uncle, "and thou dost well. But remember, without I had done so well, lad, thou hadst not risen thus. And what," added my uncle, sniggering, "will the Brüderl say when he hears the news—hey, nephew Basil?"

I had thought of that myself: it was another glorious pull over the renegade!

Whereupon my uncle—it was surely the proud fiend himself bent upon my destruction—fell to telling me I must write to my family at once, that the letter might be despatched in the morning.

I protested. I was bound to secrecy, I told him. But he scowled, and would have it that I must remember my duty to my mother, and he further made me a very long sermon upon the curses that will befall a bad child. And thus egged on — and what could I do? — I indited a very flaming document indeed, and under the seal of the strictest confidence made my poor mother acquainted with all the greatness her son was bringing into his family, and bade her rejoice with him.

The night was well worn when I had finished, and the bottle of potent Burgundy was nearly out too. Then, meaning to rise and withdraw, I fell asleep in my chair. It was grey dawn before I awoke, and I was cold as I stretched myself and staggered to my feet. In the weird thin light my uncle's face now shone out drawn and austere, with something of the look I remembered it to have borne in death.

But it was the dawn of my wedding-day, and I went to my bed — stumbling over old János, who sat, the faithful dog! asleep on the threshold — to dream of my wedding . . . a wedding with royal pomp, to the blare of trumpets and the acclamations of a multitude:

"Jennico hoch — hoch dem edlen Jennico!"

The village of Wilhelmsdhal is quite an hour's drive (even at the pace of my good horses) along the downhill road which leads from my uplifted mansion into the valley land; it takes two hours for the return way.

For safety's sake I made the announcement of my approaching marriage to the household as late in the day as possible, and, though sorely tempted to betray the exalted rank of the future mistress to the astonished major-domo, to whom János, with his usual imperturbability, interpreted my commands, I refrained, with a sense that the impression created would only after all be heightened if the disclosure were withheld till the actual apparition of the newly-made wife.

But in the vain arrogance of my delight I ordered every detail of the reception which was to greet us, and which I was determined should be magnificent enough to make up for the enforced hole-and-corner secrecy of the marriage ceremony.

Schultz the factor, my chief huntsman, and the highest among my people were to head torch-light processions of their particular subordinates at stated places along the avenue that led upwards to the house. There was to be feasting and music in the courtyard. Flowers were to be strewn from the very threshold of her new home to the door of my Princess's bridal chamber.

God knows all the extravagance I planned! It makes me sick now to think back on it!

And the wedding! Ah! that was a wedding to be proud of!

It was a dull and cloudy evening, with a high, moist wind that came in wild gusts, sweeping over the plains and tearing the leaves from the forest trees, bringing with it now a swift moonlit clearing upon the lowering face of heaven, now only thicker darkness and torrents of rain. It was all but night already in the forest roads when I started, and quite night as I emerged from out of the shelter of the mountains into the flat country. János sat on the box and my chasseurs hung on behind, and my four horses kept up a splendid pace upon the level ground. I had dressed very fine, as became a bridegroom; but fortunate it was that I had brought a dark cloak with me, for a fearful burst of storm-rain came down upon me as I jumped out from the carriage at the church door. And indeed, despite that protection, my fine white satin clothes were splashed with mud, my carefully powdered queue sadly disarranged in the few steps I had to take before reaching shelter, for the wind blew a very hurricane, and the rain came down like the rain of the deluge.

The church porch was lit only by an ill-trimmed wick floating in a saucer of oil; but by the flickering light, envious and frail as it was, I discerned at once the figure of Mademoiselle Ottilie's nurse awaiting us. Without a word she beckoned to me to follow her into the church.

The place struck cold and damp with a death-like closeness after the warm blustering air I had just left. It was even darker than the porch outside, its sole illumination proceeding from the faint glow of the little sanctuary lamp and the sullen yellow flame of two or three tallow candles stuck on spikes before a rough wooden statue on a pillar at one side. I, flanked by János and his two satellites, followed the gaunt figure to the very altar rails, where, with an imperious gesture, she signed to me to take my place.

Before turning to go she stood still a second looking at me, and methought — or it may have been a fancy born of the dismal place and the dismal gloom — that I had never seen a human countenance express so much hatred as did that woman's in the mysterious gleam of the lamp. My heart contracted with an omen of forthcoming ill.

Then I heard her feet go down the aisle, the

door open and close, and we were left alone. In the silence of the church — the most poverty-stricken and desolate, the most miserable, the most ruined to be yet used as the House of God, I think I had ever entered — at the foot of the altar of my faith, a sudden misgiving seized upon me. How would all this end? I was going to bind myself for life with the most solemn vows. Would all the honour and glory of the alliance compensate me for the loss of my liberty?

I was only twenty-six, and I knew of her who was henceforth to be my second self no more, rather less, than I knew of any of the bare-footed maids that slipped grinning about the passages of Tollendhal. To be frank with myself, the glamour of gratified vanity once stripped from before the eye of my inmost soul, what was the naked, hideous truth? I had no more love for her — man for woman — than for rosy Kathi or black-browed Sarolta!

Here my reflections were broken in upon by that very patter of naked soles that had been in my thoughts, and a little ragged boy, in a dilapidated surplice, ran round the sanctuary from some back door, and fell to lighting a pair of candles on the altar, a proceeding which only seemed once more to heighten the darkness. Presently, in a surplice and cassock as tattered as his acolyte's, with long white hair lying unkempt upon his shoulders, an old priest — in sooth, the oldest man I have ever seen alive, I believe — came forth with tottering steps; before him the tattered urchin, behind him a sacristan well-nigh as antique as himself, and as utterly pauperised.

These were to be the ministers of my grand marriage!

But almost immediately a fresh clamour of opening doors, and a light, sedate footfall, struck my ear, and all doubt and dismay disappeared like magic. Closely enveloped in the folds of a voluminous dark velvet cloak, with its hood drawn forward over her head, and beneath this shade her face muffled in the gathers of a white lace veil, I knew the stately height of my bride as she advanced towards me — and the sight of her, the sound of her brave step, set my heart dancing with the old triumph.

She stood beside me, and as the words were spoken I thought no more of the mean surroundings, of the evil omens, of the responsibilities and consequences of my act. It was nothing to me now that the old priest who wedded us, and his companion who ministered to him, should look more like mouldering corpses than living men —

that the nurse's burning eyes should still seek my face with evil look. I had no thought to spare for the position of my bride herself — her filial disobedience, her loneliness — no feeling of tenderness for the touching character of her confidence in me — no doubt as to her future happiness as my wife, nor as to my capacity for compensating her for the sacrifice of so much. I did not wonder at, nay, notice even, the absence of the lady-in-waiting — that moving spirit of our courtship. My whole soul was possessed with triumph. I was self-centred on my own success. The words were spoken; my voice rang out boldly, but hers was the barest breath of speech behind her muffling drapery. I slipped the ring (it had been my aunt's), with a passing wonder that it should prove so much too large, upon the slender finger, that hardly protruded from a fall of enveloping lace.

We were drenched with a perfect shower of holy water out of a tin bucket; and then, man and wife, we went to the sacristy to sign our names by the light of one smoking tallow candle.

I dashed mine forth with splendid flourish — the good old name of Jennico of Farringdon Dane and Tollendhal, all my qualifications, territorial, military, and inherited. And she penned hers in the flowing handwriting I already knew, Marie Ottilie:

the lofty, simple signature, as I thought with swelling heart, of sovereigns!

I pressed into the old priest's cold fingers, as he peered at us from the book, right and left, with dull, bewildered eyes, in which I thought to see the dawn of a vague misgiving, a purse bulging with notes to the value of double the sum promised; and then, with her hand upon my arm, I led her to my carriage.

The rain had begun again and the wind was storming when we drove off, my wife and I. And for a little while — a long time it seemed to me — there was silence between us, broken only by the beating of the drops against the panes of the carriage, and the steady tramp of my horses' hoofs on the wet road. Now that I had accomplished my wish, a strange embarrassment fell upon me. I had no desire to speak of love to the woman I had won. I had won her, I had triumphed — that was sufficient. I would not have undone my deed for the world; but none the less the man who finds himself the husband and has never been the lover is placed in a singular position.

I looked at the veiled figure beside me and wondered at its stillness. The light of the little lantern inside the carriage flickered upon the crimson of the velvet cloak and the white folds of the veil that hid her face from me. Then I awoke to the consciousness of the sorry figure I must present in her eyes, and, drawing from my pocket a ring, — the richest I had been able to find among my aunt's rich store, — I took the hand that lay half hidden and passive beside me, meaning to slip the jewel over the plain gold circlet I had already placed upon it. Now, as I took the hand into my own, I was struck with its smallness, its slenderness, its lightness; I remembered that even in the dark church, and with but the tips of the fingers resting in my own, a similar impression had vaguely struck me. I lifted it, spread out the little, long, thin fingers — too often had I kissed the dimpled firm hand of her Serene Highness not to know the difference! This was my wife's hand; there was my ring. But who was my wife?

I felt like a man in a bad dream. I do not know if I spoke or not; but every fibre of me was crying out aloud, as it were, in a frenzy. I suppose I turned, or looked; at any rate my companion, as if in answer to a question, said composedly:

"Yes, sir, it is so." At the same moment, putting up her veil with her right hand, she disclosed to me the features of Ottilie, the lady-in-waiting.

CHAPTER VII

I MUST have stared like a madman. For very fear of my own violence, I dared not move or speak. Mademoiselle Ottilie, or, to call her by her proper name, Madame de Jennico, very composedly removed her veil from her hair, pushed back her hood, and withdrew the hand which I still unconsciously clutched. Then she turned and looked at me as if waiting for me to speak first. I said in a sort of whisper:

"What does this mean?"

"It means, Monsieur de Jennico, that, for your own good, you have been deceived."

There was a little quiver in her voice. Was it fear? Was it mockery? I thought the latter, and the strenuous control I was endeavouring to put upon my seething passion of fury and bewilderment broke down. I threw up my arms, the natural gesture of a man driven beyond bounds, and as I did so felt the figure beside me make a sudden, abrupt movement. I thought that she shrank from me — that she feared lest I, *I*, Basil Jennico, would strike *her*, a woman! This aroused me at once to a sense of my own position, and at the same time to one of bitterest contempt for her. But as I wheeled round to gaze at her, I saw that whatever charges might be laid upon her — and God knows she had wrought a singular evil upon me! — the accusation of cowardice could not be part of them. Her face showed white, indeed, in the pale light, her features set; but her eyes looked fearlessly into mine. Every line of her figure expressed the most dauntless determination. She was braced to endure, ready to face, what she had drawn upon herself. This was no craven, rather the very spirit of daring.

"In God's name," I cried, "why have you done this?"

"And did you think," she said, looking at me, I thought, with a sort of pity, "that princesses, out of fairy tales, are so ready to marry lovers of low degree, no matter how rich or how gallant? Oh, I know what you would say — that you are well-born; but for all that, princesses do not wed with such as you, sir!"

Every drop of my blood revolted against the smart of this humiliation. Stammering and protesting, my wrath overflowed my lips.

"But this deception, — this impossible, insane fraud, — what is its object? What is *your* object?

You encouraged me — you incited me. Confusion!" I cried and clasped my head. "I think I am going mad!"

"Her Serene Highness thought that she would like to see me settled in life," said my bride, with the old look of derision on her face.

I seized her hand.

"It was the Princess's plan, then?" I asked in a whisper; and it seemed to me as if everything turned to crimson before my eyes.

She met my look — and it must have been a terrible one — with the same dauntlessness as before, and answered, after a little pause, with cool deliberation :

"Yes, it was the Princess's plan."

The carriage drove on through the rain; and again there was silence between us. My pulses beat loud in my ears; I saw, as if written in fire, the whole devilish plot to humiliate me for my presumption. I saw myself as I must appear to that high-born lady — a ridiculous aspirant whose claim was too absurd even to be seriously dealt with. And she, the creature who had lent herself to my shame, without whose glib tongue and pert audacious counsels I had never presumed, who had dared to carry out, smiling, so gross a fraud, to wear my ring and front me still — how was I to deal with her?

These were the thoughts that surged backwards and forwards in my mind, futile wreckage on a stormy sea, in the first passion of my anger.

"You know," I said at last, and felt like a man who touches solid earth at last, "that this is no marriage."

Her countenance expressed at this the most open amazement and the most righteous indignation.

"How, sir," she cried — "has not the priest wedded us? Are we not of the same faith, and does not the same Church bind us? Have not we together received a most solemn sacrament? Have not you, Basil, and I, Marie Ottilie, sworn faith to each other until death do us part? You may like it or not, Monsieur de Jennico, but we are none the less man and wife, as fast as Church can make us."

As she spoke she smiled again, and looked at me with that dimple coming and going beside the curve of her lip.

As they say men do at the point of some violent death, so I saw in the space of a second my whole life stretched before me, past and future.

I saw the two alternatives that lay to my hand, and their full consequences.

I knew what the audacious little deceiver beside me ignored — that it rested upon my pleasure alone to acknowledge or not the validity of this marriage. Let me take the step which as a man of honour I ought to take, which as a Jennico and my uncle's heir I was pledged in conscience to take, it was to hold myself up to universal mockery — and I should lay bare before a grinning world the whole extent of my pretensions and their requital.

On the other hand, let me keep my secret for a while and seemingly accept my wife: the whole point of the cursed jest would fail.

Let me show the Princess that my love for her was not so overpowering, nor my disappointment so heart-breaking, but that I had been able to find temporary compensation in the substitute with whom she had herself provided me. There are more souls lost, I believe, through the fear of ridicule than through all the temptations of the world, the flesh, and the devil!

My resolution was promptly taken: my revenge would be more exquisite and subtle than the trick that had been played upon me.

I would take her to my home, this damsel whom no feeling of maidenly restraint, of womanly compassion, had kept from acting so base a part; and for a while, at least, not all the world should guess but that in winning her my dearest wish had been accomplished. Afterwards, when I had tamed that insolent spirit, when I had taught this wild tassel-gentle to come to my hand and fly at my bidding — and I smiled to myself as I laid that plan which was full as cruel as the deception that had been practised upon me, and which I am ashamed to set out in black and white before me now — afterwards, when I chose to repudiate the woman who had usurped my name through the most barefaced imposture, if I knew the law both of land and Church, I could not be gainsaid. I had warned her that this marriage was no marriage. What could a gentleman do more?

A sudden calmness fell over me; it struck me that the laugh would be on my side after all.

My companion was first to speak. She settled herself in the corner of the carriage something like a bird that settles down in its nest, and, still with her eyes, which now looked very dark in the uncertain light, fixed upon me, said in a tone of the utmost security:

"You can beat me of course, if you like, and you can murder me if you are very, very angry; but you cannot undo what is done. I am your wife!" She gave a little nod which was the perfection of impudence. She was like some wild thing of the woods that has never seen a human being before, and is absolutely fearless because of its absolute ignorance. I ought to have pitied her, seeing how young, how childish, she was. But though there sprang into my heart strange feelings, and that dimple tempted me more and more, there was no relenting in my angry soul. Only I told myself that my revenge would be sweet. And I was half distraught, I think, between the conflict of pride, disappointment, and the strange alluring charm that this being who had so betrayed me was yet beginning to have upon me.

The speed of our four horses was slackening; we were already on the mountain road which led to my castle. There was a glimmer of moon again, the rain-beat was silent on the panes, and I could see from a turning in the road the red gleam of the torch-bearers whom I had ordered for the bridal welcome.

The monstrous absurdity of the situation struck me afresh, and my resolution grew firmer. How could I expose myself, a poor tricked fool, to the eyes of that people who regarded me as something not unlike a demi-god? No, I would keep the woman. She had sought me, not I her. I would keep her for a space at least, and let no man suspect that she was not my choice. And then, in the ripeness of time, when I would sell this old rook's nest and betake me home to England as a dutiful nephew, why, then my lady Princess should have her maid of honour back again, and see if she would find it so easy to settle her in life once more! What pity should I have upon her who had no pity for me, who had sold her maiden pride in such a sordid barter for a husband? This was no mere tool of a woman's scorn. No! Contemned by her I had wooed, played with, no doubt I had been; but I had seen enough of the relations of the two girls not to know well who was the moving spirit in all their actions. This lady had had an eye to her own interests while lending herself to my humiliation. Thinking upon it now with as cool a brain as I might,—and once I had settled upon my resolve, the first frenzy of my rage died away,—I told myself that the new Madam Jennico lied when she said it was altogether the Princess's plan; and indeed I afterwards heard from her own lips that in this I had guessed but a third of the actual truth.

And now, as we were drawing close to the first post where my over-docile and zealous retainers were already raising a fearful clamour, and I must perforce assume some attitude to face the people, I turned to my strange bride, and said to her:

"Do you think, then, it is the right of a husband to strike or slay his wife? If so, I marvel that you should have been so eager to enter upon the wedded state."

She put out her hand to me, and for the first time her composure wavered. The tears welled into her eyes and her lip quivered.

"No," she said; "and therefore I chose you, Monsieur de Jennico, not for your fine riches, not for your pedigree,"—and here, the little demon! it seemed she could not refrain from a malicious smile under the very mist of her tears,—"but because you are an Englishman, and incapable of harshness to a woman."

"And so," said I, not believing her disinterested asseveration a whit, but with a queer feeling at my heart at once bitterly angry at each word that betrayed the determination of her deceit and her most unwomanly machinations, and yet, and yet strangely melted to her, "it is reckoning on my weak good-nature that you have played me this trick?"

"No, sir," she said, flushing, "I reckoned on your manliness." And then she added, with the most singular simplicity: "I liked you, besides, too well to see you unhappily married, and the other Ottilie would have made you a wretched wife."

I burst out laughing, for, by the manes of my great-uncle, the explanation was comic! And she fell to laughing too, — my servants must have thought we were a merry couple! And, as she laughed and I looked at her, knowing her now my own, and looking at her therefore with other eyes, I deemed I had never seen a woman laugh to such bewitching purpose! And though I was full of my cruel intent, and though I dubbed her false and shameless and as deceitful a little cat as ever a man could meet, yet the dimple drew me, and I put my arms around her and kissed it. *As my lips touched hers I knew I was a lost man!*

The next moment we were surrounded with a tribe of leaping peasants, the horses were plunging, torches were waving and casting shadows upon the savage, laughing faces. If I had cursed myself for my happy thought before, I cursed myself still more now; but the situation had to be accepted. And the way in which my bride, blushing crimson from my kiss, — she who had no blush to spare for herself before this night, adapted herself to it was a marvel to me, as indeed all that I was to see or learn of her during our brief moon of wedded life was likewise to prove.

I am bound to say that the Princess herself could not have behaved with a better grace than this burgher daughter amid the wild peasants and their almost Eastern fashion of receiving their liege lady.

Within a little distance of the house it became impossible to advance with the carriage, and we were fain to order a halt and alight all in the stormy wind, and proceed on foot through the throng which had gathered thick and close about the gates, and which even Schultz's stout cane failed to disperse. My wife — I did not call her so then in my mind, but now I can call her by no other name — my wife passed through them as if she had done nothing all her life but receive the homage of the people. She gave her hand to be kissed to half a hundred fierce lips; she smiled at the poor women who clutched the hem of her gown and knelt before her. The flush my kiss had called into being had not yet faded from her cheek; there was a light in her eye, a smile upon her lip. As I looked at her and watched I could not but admit that there was no need for me to feel ashamed of her, that night.

I had sworn to give my bride a royal reception, and a royal reception she received.

Schultz had generously carried out his instructions. We sat down to a sumptuous meal which would not have misbefitted the Emperor himself. I could not eat. The acclamations and the rejoicings struck cold upon my ear. But the bride — enigma to me then as now — sat erect in her great chair at the other end of the great table, and smiled and drank and feasted daintily, and met my eye now and again with as pretty and as blushing a look as if I had chosen her among a thousand. The gipsies played their maddening music — the music of my dream — and the cries in the courtyard rose now and then to a very clamour of enthusiasm. Schultz, with a truly German sentimentality, had presented his new mistress with a large bouquet of white flowers. The smell of them turned me faint. I knew that in the great room beyond, all illuminated by a hundred wax candles, was the portrait of my uncle, stern and solitary. I would not have dared to go into that room that night to have met the look of his single watchful eye.

And yet, O God! how are we made and of what strange clay! What would I not give now to be back at that hour! What would I not give to see her there at the head of my board once more! What is all the world to me — what all the traditions of my family — what even the knowledge of her deceit and my humiliation, compared with the waste and desolation of my life without her!

CHAPTER VIII

AND now what I must set down of myself is so passing strange that had I not, I myself, lived through it, were I not now in an earthly hell for the mere want of her, I could not have believed that human nature — above all the superior quality of human nature appertaining to Basil Jennico — could be so weak a thing.

I had meant to be master: I found myself a slave! And slave of what? A dimple, a pair of yellow eyes, veiled by long black lashes — a saucy child!

I had meant to have held her merely as my toy, at the whim of my will and pleasure: and behold! the very sound of her voice, the fall of her light foot, would set my blood leaping; under the glance of her wilful eye my whole being would become as wax to the flame.

In olden days people would have said I was bewitched.

I think, looking back on it all now, that it was perhaps her singular dissimilarity from any other woman I had ever met that began the spell. Had she opposed to my anger, on that memorable night of our marriage, the ordinary arms of a woman discovered; had she wept, implored, bewailed her fate, who shall say that, even at the cost of my vanity, I might not have driven her straight back to her Princess? Who shall say that I should have wished to keep her, even to save myself from ridicule? It is impossible for me now to unravel the tangled threads of that woof that has proved the winding-sheet of my young happiness; but this I know — this of my baseness and my better nature — that once I had kissed her I was no longer a free man. And every day that passed, every hour I spent beside her, welded closer and firmer the chains of my servitude.

She was an enigma which I ever failed to solve. That alone was alluring. Judged by her actions, most barefaced little schemer, most arrant adventuress plotting for a wealthy match, there was yet something about her which absolutely forbade me to harbour in her presence an unworthy thought of her. Guilty of deceit such as hers had been towards me, she ought to have displayed either a conscience-stricken or a brazen soul: I found her emanate an atmosphere not only of childlike innocence but of lofty purity that often made me blush for my grosser imaginings.

She ought, by rights, to have feared me — to have been humble at least: she was as proud as Lucifer before the fall and as fearless as he when he dared defy his Creator. She ought to have mistrusted me, shown doubt of how I would treat her: and alas! in what words could I describe the confidence she gave me? so generous, so sublime, so guileless. It would have forced one less enamoured than myself into endeavouring to deserve it for very shame!

A creature of infinite variety of moods, with never a sour one among them; the serenest temper and the merriest heart I have ever known; a laugh to make an old man young, and a smile to make a young man mad; as fresh as spring; as young and as fanciful! I never knew in what word she would answer me, what thing she would do, in what humour I should find her. Yet her tact was exquisite. She dared all and never bruised a fibre (till that last terrible day, my poor lost love!). And besides and beyond this, there was yet another thing about her which drew me on till I was all lost in love. She was elusive. I never felt sure of her, never felt that she was wholly mine. Her tenderness — oh, my God, her tenderness! — was divine, and yet I felt I had not all she had to give. There was still a secret hanging upon that exquisite lip, a mystery that I had yet to solve, a land that lay unexplored before me. And it comes upon me like madness, now that she is gone from me, perhaps for ever, that I may never know the word of the riddle.

I have said that the past is like a dream to look back upon; no part of it is more dreamlike than the days which followed my strange wedding. They seemed to melt into each other, and yet it is the memory of them which is at once my joy and my torture now.

At first she did not touch, nor did I, upon the question which lay like a covered fire always smouldering between us; and in a while it came about with me that I lived as a gambler upon the pleasure of the moment. And though in my heart I had not told myself yet that I would give up my revenge, — though it was hidden there, a sleeping viper, cruel and implacable, — I strove to forget it, strove to think neither of the future nor of the past. I hung a curtain over my uncle's picture, at which old János nearly broke his heart. I rolled up the pedigree very tight and rammed it into a drawer . . . and the autumn days seemed all too short for the golden hours they gave me.

No one came to disturb us in our solitude, no hint from the outer world. We two were as apart in our honeymoon as the most jealous lovers could wish. I knew not what had become of the Princess. In very truth I could not bear to think of her; the memory of the absurd part I had been made to play was so unpalatable, was associated with so much that was painful and humiliating, and brought with it such a train of disquieting reflections that I drove it from me systematically. I never wanted to see the woman again, to hear her voice, or even learn what had become of her. That I never had one particle of lover's love for her was plainer than ever to me now, in the midst of the new feelings with which my unsought bride inspired me. I knew what love meant at last, and would at times be filled with an angry contempt for myself, that she who had proved herself so all unworthy should be the one to have this power upon me.

Thus the days went by quite aimlessly. And by-and-by as they went the thought of what I had planned to do became less and less welcome to me, not (to my shame be it said) for its wickedness, but because I could not contemplate life without my present happiness. And after yet a while the idea (at first rejected as monstrous, impossible, nay, even as a base breach of faith to my dead uncle) that I might make the sacrifice of my Jennico pride and actually content myself after all with this unfit alliance, began to take shape within me. Gradually this idea grew dearer to me hour by hour, though I still in secret held to the possibility of my other plan, as a sort of "rod in pickle" over the head of my perverse companion, and caressed it now and again in my inmost soul — when she was most provoking — as a method to bring her to my knees in dire humiliation, but only to have the ultimate sweetness of nobly forgiving her. For Ottilie was far from showing a proper spirit of contrition or a fitting sense of what she owed me; and this galled me at times to the quick. I had never ceased to entertain the resolve of taming the wild little lady, although I found it increasingly difficult to begin the process.

Alone we were by no means lonely, even though the days fell away into a month's length. We rode together, we drove, we walked; she chattered like a magpie, and I never knew a second's dulness. She whipped my blood for me like a frosty wind, and, or so it seemed to me, took a new bloom, a new beauty in her happiness. For she was happy. The only sour visage in Tollendhal at the time was, I think, that of the strange nurse. I had found her waiting in my wife's bedroom the night of our home-coming. She never spoke to me during the whole time of her stay, nor to Schultz, although he was her countryman. With the others, of course (saving János) she could not have exchanged a word, and but that she spoke with her mistress sometimes, I should have thought her dumb. That woman hated me. I have seen her eyes follow me about as if she would willingly murder me; but her nursling she loved in quite as vehement a fashion, and therefore I bore with her.

We had been married a week when Ottilie first made allusion to the Princess. We were to ride out on that day, and she came down to breakfast all equipped but for one boot.

I have never seen so daintily untidy a person as she was in all my life. Her hair smelt of fresh violets, but there was always a twist out of place, or a little curl that had broken loose. Her clothes were of singular fineness and richness, but she would tear them and tatter them like a very schoolgirl romp. And so that morning she tripped in with one pink satin bedroom slipper and one yellow leather riding boot. I would not let her send for her dark-visaged attendant to repair the neglect, but fetched the boot myself and knelt to put it on. As I took off the slipper I paused for a moment weighing it in my hand. It was so little a thing, so slender, so pretty! She looked down at me with a smile, and said composedly:

"Do you think, sir, that the other Ottilie could have put on that shoe?"

It was, as I said, the first time that the subject had been mentioned between us since the night of our marriage. I felt as if a cloud came over me, and looked up darkly at her. It was not wise, surely, I thought in my heart, to touch upon what I was willing to forget. But she had no misgiving. She slipped out from under her long riding skirt the small unbooted foot in its shining pink silk stocking, and said:

"You would *not* have liked, Monsieur de Jennico, to have acted lady's-maid to her, for you are very fastidious, as it did not take me long to find out. Oh," she went on, "if you knew how grateful you ought to be to me for preventing you from marrying her! You would have been so unhappy, and you deserved a better fate."

"But I thought," said I — and such was my weakness that the sight of her pretty foot took away my anger, and I was all lost in the discovery of how everything about her seemed to curve: her hair in its ripples, her lip in its arch, her nostrils, her little chin, her lithe young waist, and now, her foot — "I thought," and as I spoke

I took it into my hand, "it was the Princess's plan."

"Did I say so?" she said lightly. "That woman was never capable of a plan in her life! No, sir, I always made her do what I liked. Her intelligence was just brilliant enough to allow her to realise that she had better follow my advice. Will you put on my boot, sir? Ah! what treachery." I held her tightly by the heel and looked up well pleased at her laughing face — I loved to watch her laugh — and then I kissed her silk stocking and put the boot on. To such depths had I come in my unreasoning infatuation. I felt no anger with her for the revelation which, indeed, as I think I have previously set down, was from the beginning scarcely news to me. I had yet to learn how completely innocent of all complicity in the deception played upon me was her poor Serenity, how innocent even of the pride and contempt I still attributed to her!

The season for the chase had opened; once or twice I had already been out with the keepers after stags, or wild boars, and my wife, a pretty figure in her three-cornered hat and fine green riding suit, had ridden courageously at my side. At the beginning of the third week we made a journey higher into the mountains and stayed a few days at a certain hunting-box, the absolute isolation of which seemed by contrast to make Tollendhal a very vortex. The wild place pleased her fancy. We had some splendid boar-hunting in the almost inaccessible passes of the mountains, and Ottilie showed herself as keen at the chase as I, although, woman-like, she shrank from the finish. She vowed she loved the loneliness, the simplicity, of the rough wood-built lodge, the savageness of the scenery. She loved too the novel excitement of the life, the long day's riding, the sleepy supper by the roaring wood fire, with the howl of the dogs outside, and the cry of the autumn wind about the heights. She begged me with pretty insistence that we should come back and spend the best part of the coming month in this airy nest.

"We are more alone," she said coaxingly, with one of her rare fits of tenderness. "You are more mine, Basil." And I promised her that we should only return to Tollendhal to settle matters with the steward and provide ourselves with what we wanted, and then that we should have a new honeymoon. I would have promised anything at such a moment. It is the truth that in those days, somehow, we had, as she said, grown closer to each other.

On the last night, wearied out by the long hours on horseback, she had fallen asleep as she sat in a great carved wooden chair by the flaming hearth, while I sat upon the other side, wakeful, watching her, full of thought. She looked all a child as she slept, her face small and pale and tired, the shadow of the long lashes very black upon her cheeks. And then came upon me like a sort of nightmare the memory of what I had meant to make of this young creature who had trusted herself to me. For the first time I faced my future boldly, and took a great resolve in the silence, listening to the fall of her light breath, and the sullen roar of the wind in the pine forest without.

I resolved to sacrifice my pride and keep my low-born wife.

CHAPTER IX

It was full of this resolve, with an uplifted consciousness of my own virtue, that I started next morning beside her upon our homeward way. The day was very bright; and the bare trees, with here and there a yellow or red leaf, showed against a sky of palest blue. There was a frost about us, and our horses were fresh and full of pranks, as we wound down the rocky paths. My wife, too, was in a skittish humour, which irritated me a little as being ill-assorted to my own high-strung feelings and my secret sense of magnanimity. She mocked at my solemn face, she sang ends of silly songs to herself. I would have spoken to her of what was on my heart; I would have had her grateful to me, conscious of her own sin and my generosity. But I could get her to hearken to no serious speech. She called me "Monsieur de la Faridondaine," and plucked a bunch of ash berries as we rode, and stuck them over one ear, and asked me, her face dimpling, if it was not becoming to her. And then, when I still urged that I would talk of grave matters, she pulled a grimace, and fell to mimicking Schultz with "Jawohl, Gnädigster Herr," till I was fain to laugh with her and put off my sermon till the audience was better disposed.

But my heart was something sore against her. And when we reached home, I found *that* awaiting me which awoke a flame of the fierce resentment of the first hour of discovery. It was a letter from my mother in answer to the wild, inflated, triumphant lucubration I had sent her on the eve of my wedding-day. I had, of course, not attempted to undeceive her — in fact, as I have already set down, it was only within the last twenty-four hours that I had settled upon a definite plan of action. My dear mother, who dearly loved, as she herself admitted, the princes of this earth, was in a tremendous flutter at my exalted alliance. I read her words, her proud congratulations, with a feeling of absolute nausea. My brother, she wrote, was torn betwixt a sense of the increased family importance and the greenest envy, that I, who had paid no price of honour for the gaining of them, should have risen to such heights of grandeur and wealth. Not hearing from me since the great announcement, she had ventured (so she confessed) to confide my secret to a few dear friends, and " it had got about strangely," she added naïvely. The whole Catholic world, the whole English world of fashion, was ringing with the news of the great Jennico match. In fact, the poor lady was as nearly beside herself with pride and glory when she wrote to me, as I had been when I gave her the news. I did not — I am glad to say this — I did not for a second waver in my resolution of fidelity to my wife, but I told myself, with an intolerable sense of injury, that I could never face the shame of returning to England again; that the full sacrifice entailed upon me was not only the degradation of an unsuitable alliance, but that hardest of trials to the true-blooded Englishman, perpetual expatriation!

In this grim and bitter temper I marched into the room where I now sit, and drew back the curtain from my uncle's picture and took forth the pedigree from its hidden recess. The old man wore, as I knew he would, a most severe countenance.

But I turned my back upon him in a disrespectful fashion I had never dared display during his life, and spread out again that fateful roll of parchment on the table before me, while with penknife and pumicestone I sought to efface all traces of that vainglorious entry that mocked me in its clear black and white. The blood was surging in my head and singing in my ears, when I heard a light step, and looking up saw Ottilie. She could not have come at a worse moment. She held letters in her hand, which upon seeing me she thrust into her pocket with a sly look and something of a blush. She too, it seemed, had found a courier awaiting her; the secretness of the action stirred the heat of my feelings against her yet more. But I strove to be calm and judicial.

"Ottilie," I said, "come here. I have to converse with you on matters of importance."

She drew near me, pouting and with a lagging step, like a naughty child.

"That sacred pedigree," she said, and thrust out her under-lip. She spoke in French, which gave the words altogether a different meaning, and in my then humour I was hugely shocked to hear such an expression from her lips.

"You behave strangely," I said, with coldness, not to be mollified by the half-pleading, half-mischievous glance she cast upon me, "and you speak like a child. There has been enough of childishness, enough of folly, in this business. It is time to be serious," I said, and struck the table with my flat palm as I spoke.

"Well, let us be serious," she retorted, slapping the table too, and then sat down beside me, propping her chin upon her hands in her favourite attitude. "Am I not serious?" she proceeded, looking at me with a face of mock solemnity. "Well, Mr. my husband, what do you wish of me?"

"Have you ever thought, Ottilie," said I, "of the position you have placed me in? I have been obliged to-day to come to a grave resolution — I have had to make up my mind to give up my country and remain here for the rest of my life. It is in direct defiance to my uncle's commands and last wishes, and it is no pleasant thing to an Englishman to give up his native land."

"If so, why do it?" she said coolly. "I am quite willing to go to England. In fact, I should rather like it."

"Because, before heaven, madam," said I, irritated beyond bounds, "you have left me no other alternative. Do you think I am going home to be a laughing-stock among my people?"

"Then," she said with lightning quickness, "you broke your promise of secrecy. It is your own fault: you should have kept your word."

Struck by the irrefutable truth of this remark, although at the same time my wrath was secretly accumulating against her for this systematic indifference to her own share in a transaction where she was the chief person to blame, I kept silence for a moment, drumming with my fingers on the table.

"Eh bien!" she said at last, with a note of amusement and tender indulgence in her voice as a mother might speak to her unreasonable infant. "This terrible resolution taken, what follows? You have effaced, I see, your entry in the famous pedigree, and you would now fill it up with the detail of your real alliance? Is that it?"

I glanced up at her: her eyes were dancing with an eager light, her lip trembling as if over some merry word she yet forbore to speak. Her want of sympathy in sight of my evident distress was hard to bear.

"Yes," I answered, "the pedigree must be filled up. I don't even know your whole name, nor who your father was, nor yet your mother. I have your word for it, however," I said, and the sentence was bitter to me to speak, "that your family was originally of burgher origin."

"Put down," she answered, "Marie Ottilie Pahlen, daughter of the deceased Herrn Geheimrath Baron Pahlen, Hof Doctor to his Serene Highness the Reigning Duke of Lausitz."

The pen dropped from my hand.

"Your father was a doctor?" I asked in an extinguished voice.

K

"Ennobled," she returned promptly, "after successfully piloting his Serene Highness through a bad attack of jaundice."

"And your mother?" I murmured, clinging yet to the hope that on the mother's side at least the connection might prove a little more worthy of the House of Jennico.

She hesitated and glanced at me. Once more I seemed to see some inner source of mirth bubble on her lip; or was it only that she was possessed by the very spirit of mischief? Anyhow, she forced her smile to gravity again and answered me steadily, while her eyes sought mine with a curious determined meaning at variance with the mock meekness of the rest of her countenance.

"Put down, Monsieur de Jennico, — 'and of Sophia Müller, likewise deceased,' and add if you like, 'once personal maid to her Serene Highness the Dowager Duchess, Marie Ottilie of Lausitz.'"

I sat like a man struck silly, and in the tide of fury that swept over me my single lucid thought was that if I spoke or moved I should disgrace myself. And she chose that moment, poor child, to come over to me and place her arms round my neck, and say caressingly in my ear:

"Write it, write it, sir, and then tell me that, seeing that I am I, and that I should not be different from myself were I the daughter of the Emperor, all this matters little to you since we love each other."

I put her from me: my hands were trembling, but I was very gentle. I brought her round to face me, and she awaited my answer with a triumphant smile. It was that smile undid me and her. She made too sure of me — she had conquered me too easily all along.

"You ask overmuch," I said when I could command my voice enough to speak, "you take overmuch for granted. You forget how you have deceived me; how you have betrayed me. I am willing," I said, "to believe you have not been all to blame, that you were encouraged and upheld by another, but this does not exonerate you from the chief share in a very questionable transaction."

The words fell cuttingly. I saw how the smile faded from her face, saw how the pretty dimple lingered a second like a pale ghost of itself, and then was lost in the droop of her lip, which trembled like a chidden babe's. And I took a cruel joy to think I had hit her at last. But in a second or two she spoke with all her old courage.

"It is well," she said, "to blame where blame is due. If you wish to blame any one for our marriage, blame me alone. The other Ottilie never received your letter; never knew you wanted to marry her; had nothing to say to what you call my betrayal of you. She would have prevented this marriage if she could. Nay, I will tell you more: I believe she might even have married you had I given her the chance. But I knew you would marry her solely because of her position, of her title; that you had no love for her beyond your insane love of her royal blood. I thought you worthy of better things; I thought you could rise above so pitiable a weakness; I thought you could learn of love that love alone is worth living for! And if you have not learned, if indeed, my scholar, you have been taught nothing in love's school, if you can lay bare your soul now and tell yourself that you would rather have had the wife you wanted in your overweening vanity than the wife I am to you, why then, sir, I have made a grievous mistake, and I am willing to acknowledge that I have committed an irrevocable wrong both to you and to myself."

Now, as she spoke, I was torn by a strange mixture of feelings, and my love for her contended with my pride, my wounded vanity, my sense of injury. I could not in truth answer that I would rather have been wedded to the Princess, for one thing had these weeks made clear to me above all things, and that was that married life with her would have been intolerable. But my anger against the woman I did love in spite of myself was not lessened by the tone of reproachful superiority she assumed; and because of the truth of her rebuke it was the harder for my self-love to bear. Before I could muster words clear enough and severe enough to answer her with, she proceeded:

"Come, Basil, come, rise above this failing which is so unworthy of you. Throw that musty old pedigree away before it eats all the manliness out of your life. What does it mean but that you can trace your family up to a greater number of probable rascals, hard and selfish old men, than another? Be proud of yourself for what you are; be proud of your forefathers, indeed, if they have done fine deeds of valour, or virtue; but this cant about birth for birth's sake, about the superiority of aristocracy as aristocracy — what does it amount to? It is to me the most foolish of superstitions. Was that old man," she asked, pointing to my uncle, who frowned upon her murderously — "was that old man a better man than his heiduck János? Was he a braver soldier? Was he a better servant to *his* master? Was he more honest in his dealings? shrewder in his counsel?

I tell you I honour János as much as I would have honoured him. I tell you that if I love you, I love you for what you are, not because you are descended from some ignorant savage king, not because you can boast that the blood of the worst of men and sovereigns, the most profligate, the most treacherous, the most faithless, Charles Stuart, runs in your veins — I hope, sir, as little of it as possible."

I sprang to my feet. To be thus rated by her who should be kneeling for forgiveness! It was intolerable.

"I think," I thundered, "that, considering your position, a little humility would be more becoming than this attitude! You should remember that you are here on tolerance only; that it is to my generosity alone that you owe the right to call yourself an honest woman."

"What do you mean?" said she, as fiercely as I had spoken myself.

"I mean," said I — "I mean, madam, that you are what I choose to make you. That marriage you so skilfully encompassed is, if I choose it, no marriage."

She put her hands to her head like one who has turned suddenly giddy.

"You married me before God's altar," she said

in a sort of whisper; "you married me, and you took me home."

I was still too angry to stay my tongue.

With a bitter laugh, "I married the Princess," I said, "but I took the servant home."

A burning tide of blood rushed to her brow; I saw it unseeing, as a man does in passion; but I have lived that scene over and over again, waking and dreaming, since, and every detail of it is stamped upon my brain. Next she grew livid white, and spread out her hands, as though a precipice had suddenly opened before her; and then she cried:

"And this is your English honour!" and turning on her heel she left me.

The scorn of her tone cut me like a whip. I swore a mighty oath that I would never forgive her till she sued for pardon. She must be taught who was master. In solitude she should reflect, and learn to rue her sins to me — her audacity — her unwarrantable presumption — her ingratitude!

All in my white heat of anger I summoned János and bade him tell his mistress's nurse that I had gone into the mountains for a week. And then I ordered a fresh horse, and followed only by the old man, dashed off like one possessed into the rocky wastes.

Alone in the solitary hut, by that hearth where but the night previous my heart had overflowed with such tenderness for her, I sat and nursed my grievances and brooded upon my wrongs till they grew to overpowering size and multiplied a thousandfold; and curious it is that what I thought of most was the bitter unfairness to me, the monstrous injustice of her contempt, at the very moment when I had meant to sacrifice my life and prospects to her. I told myself she did not love me, had never loved me, and worked myself to a pitch of frenzy over that thought. The memory of her announcement on this afternoon, the full knowledge of her deceit, the confession of her worse than burgher origin, weighed not now one feather-weight in my resentment. That I had cast from me as the least of my troubles; so can a man change and so can love swallow up all other passions! No doubt, I told myself, she was mocking me now in her own mind; no doubt she reckoned that her poor infatuated fool would come creeping back with all promptitude and beg for her smile. She should learn at last that she had married a man; not till I saw her down at my very feet would I take her back to my breast.

All next day I hunted in a bitter wind and in

a bitter temper. There were clouds arising, my huntsmen told me, that looked very like snow clouds, and I must beware being snowed up upon the height. I was in the humour to welcome hardship and even danger, and so the whole day we rode after an old rogue boar and came back in darkness, at no small risk, empty handed, and the roughness of my temper by no means improved. Next day the weather still held up, and again I hunted. My men must have wondered what had come over their erstwhile genial master. Even my uncle could not have shown them a harder rule or ridden them with less consideration through the hardest of ways in the teeth of the most fiendish of winds.

That night, again, I sat and brooded by the leaping flame of the pine logs, but it was in a different mood. All my surly determination, my righteous indignation, had melted from me, leaving me as weak as water. Of a sudden in the closest heat of the chase there had come to me an awful vision of what I had done; a terrible swift realisation of the insult I had flung at the face of the woman who was indeed the wife of my heart and love. Oh, God, what had I done? I had sought to humble her — I had but debased myself! Through the whole day her words, "Is this your English honour?" had rung a dismal rhythm in my ear to the beat of my horse's hoofs on the hard ground, to the call of the horn amid the winding rocks. The vision of her faded smile, of her dimple paled to a pitiable ghost, of her babyish drooping lip, and then of her white face struck with such scorn, haunted me to madness. I sickened from my food as I sat to my supper, and put down my cup untasted. And now as the wind whistled and the foreboded storm was gathering upon us, the longing to see her, to be with her, to kneel at her feet — yes, *I* would now be the one to kneel — came upon me with such violence that I could not withstand it.

I ordered my horses. I would listen to no remonstrance, no warning. I must return to Tollendhal, I said, were all the powers of darkness leagued against me. And return I did. It was a piece of foolhardiness in which I ran, unheeding, the risk of my life; but the Providence that protects madmen protected me that night, and János and I arrived in safety through a gale of wind and a fall of snow that might indeed have proved our death. All covered with rime I ran into the house and up to the door of her room. It was past midnight, and there I paused for a moment fearing to disturb her.

Two or three of the women came pattering down the passage to me and with expressive gestures addressed me volubly; one of the girls was weeping. I could not understand a word they said, but with a new terror I burst open the door of the bedroom. In this appalling dread I realised for the first time how I loved my wife!

The room was all empty and all dark; I called for lights. There was no trace of her presence; her bed had not been slept in. Like a maniac I tore about the house, seeking her, shrieking her name, demanding explanations from those to whom my speech meant nothing. I recked little of my dignity, little of the impression I must create upon my household! And at last János, his wrinkled face withered up and contorted with the trouble he dared not speak, gave me the tidings that the gracious lady had gone. She and her nurse had set forth on foot and left no message with any one.

What need is there for me to write down what I endured that black night? When I look back upon it it is as one may look back upon some terrible nightmare, some hideous memory of delirium. She had left me, and left me thus, without a word, and with but one sign. The cursed pedigree was still spread upon the table where we had quarrelled. I found upon it her wedding ring. A great cross had been drawn over the half-written entry of our marriage. That was all, but it was surely enough. The jewels I had given her were carefully packed in their cases and laid upon a table in her room. Her own things had been gathered together the day of her departure, which was the day I left her, and they had been fetched the next morning by some strange servant in an unknown travelling coach. More than this I have not been able to glean, for the storm has rendered the ways impassable; but it is rumoured that the Countess de Schreckendorf is dead, and that the Princess also has left the country.

I have no more to say. It is only two nights ago since I came home to such misery, and how I have passed the hours, what needs it to set forth? At times I tell myself that it is better so, that she is false and base, and that I were the poorest of wretches to forgive her. But at times again I see the whole naked truth before me, and I know that she was to me what no woman can be again. And my uncle looks down at me as I write, with a sour frowning face, and seems — strange it is, yet true — to revile me now with bitter scorn, not for having kept her, the roturière, but for having driven her from my castle!

"Thou hadst her; thou couldst not hold her," he seems to snarl.

Old man, old man, it is your teaching that has undone me; do you reproach me now that it has wrought my ruin?

Basil Jennico flung his pen from him; the logs in the hearth had burnt themselves to white ash; his candles were guttering in their sockets, and behind the close-drawn curtains the faint dawn was spreading over a world of snow. The wind still howled, the storm was still unabated.

"Another day," groaned he, "another hateful day!" He flung his arms before him and his head down upon them. So sleep came upon him; and so old János, creeping in a little later, red-eyed from his watchful night, found him. The sleeper woke as the man, with hands rough and gnarled, yet tender as a woman's, strove to lift him to an easier attitude; woke and looked at him with a fixed semi-conscious stare.

"Ottilie!" he cried wildly, and suddenly brought back to grey reality stopped and clasped his head. There was in the old servant's hard and all but immutable face so wistful a yearning of kindred sorrow that, suddenly catching sight of it in the midst of his despair, the young man broke down and fell forward like a child upon that faithful breast.

"Courage, honoured master," said János, "we will find her again."

PART II

CHAPTER I

MEMOIR OF CAPTAIN BASIL JENNICO (A PORTION, WRITTEN EARLY IN THE YEAR 1772, IN HIS ROOMS AT GRIFFIN'S, CURZON STREET)

HOME in England once again, if home it can be called, this set of hired chambers, so dreary within, with outside the lowering fog and the unfamiliar sounds that were once so familiar. It is all strange, after eight years' exile; and the grime, the noise, the narrow limits, the bustle of this great city, weary me after the noble silence, the wide life, at Tollendhal.

It was with no lightening of my thoughts that I saw the white cliffs of old England break the sullen grey of the horizon, with no patriotic joy that I set foot on my native soil again, but rather with a heavy, heavy heart. What can this land be to me now but a land of exile? All that makes home to a man I have left behind me.

I hardly know why I have resumed the thread of this miserable story. God knows that I have no good thing to narrate, and that this setting forth, this storing, as it were, of my bitter harvest of disappointments, can bring no solace with it. And yet man must hope as long as life lasts; and the hope keeps springing up again, in defiance of all reason, that, somehow, some day, we shall meet again. Therefore I write, in order that, should such a day come, she may read for herself and learn how the thought of her filled each moment of my life since our parting; that she may read how I have sought her, how I have mourned for her; that she may know that my love has never failed her.

This it is that heartens me to my task. Moreover, all else is so savourless that I know not how otherwise to fill the time. I have been here five weeks; there are many houses where I am welcome, many friends who would gladly lend me their company, many places where young men can find distraction of divers kinds and degrees; but I have not succeeded in bringing myself to take up the new life with any zest: I had rather dwell upon the past in spite of all its bitterness, than face the desolation of the present.

It was on the third day of the great storm that the pen fell from my hand at Tollendhal, and for four and twenty hours more that self-same storm raged in violence. One word of my old servant's had brought me on a sudden to a definite purpose. I was full of eager hope of tracing her, of finding her, once it were possible to start upon the quest. For the gale which kept me prisoner must have retarded her likewise; and even with two days' start, I told myself, she could not have gone far upon her road.

But I reckoned without the difficulties which the first great snowfall of the year, before the hard frost comes to make it passable for sledging, was creating for us in these heights where the drifts fill to such depth. Day and night my fellows worked to cut a way for me down to the imperial road; and I worked with them, watched, encouraged them, and all, it seemed, to so little purpose that I thought I should have gone mad outright. The cruel heavens now smiled, now frowned, upon our work, so that, between frost and thaw and thaw and frost, the task was doubled, and my prison bars seemed to grow stronger instead of less.

In this way it came to pass that it was full ten days from the time that she had left Tollendhal that I was at length able to start forth in pursuit.

My first stage was of course to the castle of the old Countess Schreckendorf, where I found the place well-nigh deserted, its mistress having been, even as I had been informed, a fortnight dead and buried. But there was a servant in charge of the empty, desolate house, and from her I gleaned tidings both precise and sufficient.

The Princess had remained quietly at Schreckendorf during the weeks which had followed upon my marriage, but on the day previous to our return to Tollendhal from the shooting-lodge, a couple of couriers had arrived at the Countess's gates close one upon the other, bringing, it would seem, important letters for the Princess, who had been greatly agitated upon receipt of them. She had hastily despatched a mounted messenger to my wife, whether with a private communication from herself or merely to forward missives addressed to her from her own home I know not; but at any rate the papers which Ottilie had hidden from me that fatal day were brought her by this man. After she left Tollendhal a few hours later, my wife had arrived at Schreckendorf in a peasant's cart. That same evening two travelling coaches, bringing ladies, officers, and servants, had made their appearance at the castle; it was one of these coaches which went to the stronghouse next morning and bore away Ottilie's belongings. In the afternoon the whole party, including my wife, had set forth in great haste for the north, despite universal warning of the gathering storm. There could be no doubt but that their destination was Lausitz, most probably the Residence itself, Budissin.

When I had ascertained all this I promptly decided upon my course. Taking with me János only, I instantly started for the next post-town, where we were able to secure fresh horses, and whence we pushed on the same night some twenty miles farther.

Not until the sixth evening, however, despite our extraordinarily hard travelling, did we, mounted upon a pair of sorry and worn-out nags, find ourselves crossing the bridge under the towered gates of Budissin. That was then the sixteenth day from the date of my wife's flight.

It seemed a singularly deserted town as we stumbled over the cobbles of the streets, with the early dusk of the November day closing in upon us — so few people passed us as we went, so few windows cast a light into the gloom, so many houses and shops presented but blank closed shutter-fronts. János knew his way, having ridden with my uncle in all this district during the late war. There was a very good inn, he told me, on the Burg Platz, in the shadow of the palace; and as nothing could suit my purpose better, to the "Silver Lion of Lusatia" we therefore turned our horses' heads.

It was cheering, after our long wayfaring, and the dismal nightmare-like impression of our passage through the empty town, to see the casements of that same "Silver Lion" shine afar off ruddily; and my heart leaped within me to discern, dimly sketched behind it, the towering outline of the palace, wherein, no doubt, my lost bird had found refuge.

The voice of the red-faced host who, at sound of clattering hoofs before his door, came bustling to greet us as fast as his goodly bulk would allow, struck on my ear with cheering omen.

"God greet ye, my lords!" he cried, as he lent a shoulder for my descent; "you are welcome this bitter night to fireside and supper. Enter, my lords; I have good wine, good beds, good supper, for your lordships, and the best beer that is brewed between Munich and Berlin. Joseph, thou rag, see to his lordship's horses; wife, come greet our worshipful visitors!"

I write down the jargon much as I heard it, for, as I write, I am back again at that moment and feel once more the glow of hope which crept into my heart, even as the genial warmth of the room unbent my frozen limbs. I had reached my journey's end, and the old rhyme in the play, "journeys end in lovers meeting," rang a merry burden in my thoughts.

I marvel now that my hopes should have been so forward; that I should have reckoned so much more upon her woman's love than upon her woman's pride. Indeed, I had not deemed my sin so great but that my penitence would amply atone. So I was all eagerness to satisfy my hungering heart by tidings of her, and could hardly sit still to my supper — though we had ridden hard and I was famished — till I had induced mine host to sit beside me and crack a bottle of his most recommended Rhenish, which should unloose a tongue that scarcely needed such inducement. For her sake, that no scandal might be bruited about her fair name, I had determined to proceed cautiously.

"You have a fine town here, friend," said I, "so far as I can judge this dark night."

"Truly, your lordship may say so," said he, and smacked his lips that I might understand how great a relish this fruit of his cellar left on a man's palate.

"But it has a deserted look," said I idly, just to encourage him in talk; "so many houses shut up — so few people about."

He rolled the wine round his mouth in a reflective manner, then swallowed it with a gulp, and threw an uneasy look at me. At the same instant there flashed upon my mind what, strange as it may seem, I had clean forgotten in the turmoil of my thoughts and the hurry of my pursuit: the reason for the very state of affairs I was commenting on — the plague of smallpox, the malady that had driven the Princess to my land! Ay, in very truth the town had a plague-stricken look, and I felt myself turn pale to think my wife had come back to this nest of infection.

"The sickness," said I then quickly, — "has it abated here? Nay, I know all about it, man, and have no fear of it. But how fares it in the town and in the palace?"

"Oh, the sickness!" quoth mine host with a great awkward laugh. "His lordship means these few little cases of smallpox. Na, it had been nothing, and is all over now; only folk were such cowards and frightened themselves sick, and families fled because of this same foolish fear. Now myself, as his lordship sees, myself and my family and my servants, we have not known a day's ill-health, because we kept our hearts up and drank good stuff. 'It is,' as I said to his Highness himself, who never left the place, but went out in our midst, the noble prince, and spat at fear (besides that he had already had it, like myself),—'it is the wine,' said I, 'or the beer, if you know where to get it, that keeps a man sound.' And his Highness says to me——"

But here I interrupted the speaker in a voice the trembling of which I could not control.

"Is the Duke at the palace now, then, with all his household?"

"He has been so, my lord," said the man eagerly, "up to the last week; so long, indeed, as there was a suspicion of illness among us. But now he is at the summer castle, Ottilienruhe, near Rothenburg. 'Tis but three leagues from the town. The Princess, sir, is always fond of Ottilienruhe, even in this cold weather. And as she has but just returned from visiting at another Court, his Highness, her father, has gone to join her thither. Our Princess, sir, is a most beautiful young lady; nay, if you will allow me, I will show you a portrait of her, which we have framed in my wife's room. A beautiful young lady, sir! There will be rare festivities when she weds her cousin, the Margrave of Liegnitz-Rothenburg. We have his portrait, too — a very noble gentleman! I would show you these pictures; I think you would admire them."

But I arrested him with a gesture, as, in the hopes of distracting my attention from an awkward topic, he was about to roll his bulk in quest of these treasures.

I had no wish, indeed, to feast my eyes upon that face, the lineaments of which, with all their beauty, I could not bear to recall. What was it to me whom *that* Ottilie married? If they had had a portrait of my Ottilie, indeed! . . . But, sweet soul, she had told me herself of her obscurity and unimportance.

"And so," said I, "they are at the summer palace, your reigning family?"

And though I had hugged the thought of her dear living presence so close to me this night, behind yonder palace walls, I nevertheless rejoiced to learn that she was safer harboured.

"The Princess has her retinue with her, I suppose?"

"Oh, ay," said the innkeeper, rising as he spoke and clacking his tongue again over the last drop of his wine. "Though our Princess is so simple a lass, if I may say so without disrespect, and loves not Court fashions. But she has one favourite companion, and they are as sisters together, so that when one sees her Highness, one may be sure the Fräulein is not far distant. Oh, ay, sir, they have returned from their travels together, though I have heard it rumoured that one or two of her Highness's attendants have been left behind, dead or ailing. Na, it is better to stay at home: strange places are unwholesome!"

He opened the stove door and shoved in two or three great logs, and I turned and stretched my limbs to the warmth with lazy content, and, for the first time for many a long day and night, a restful heart.

To-morrow I should see her. When I slept that night I dreamed golden dreams.

The next day dawned upon a world all involved in creeping grizzling mist, that seemed to ooze even into the comfortable rooms of the "Silver Lion"; that wrapped from my view the lofty towers of the palace beyond my window, and damped even my buoyant confidence. My good János had the toothache, and though it was not in him to complain, the sight of his swollen, suffering face did not further encourage me to cheer.

A little before noon we mounted to ride forth to Ottilienruhe in the dismal weather. Our garments, despite the heiduck's endless brushing, bore many traces of our hard journey. We cut but a poor figure, I thought, in these stained, rusty clothes; and the young lord of Tollendhal was ill-mounted upon the wretched jade, which had, nevertheless, faithfully served him upon his last cruel stage. The poor nag was yet full weary, and stumbled and drooped her head, while János's white-faced bay might have stood for the very image of starving antiquity.

I winced as I thought of Ottilie's mocking glance; but the haste to see her overcame even my delicate vanity.

Following my host's directions, who marvelled greatly at our eccentricity that we should leave a warm stove door and good cheer from mere travellers' curiosity on such a day, we pattered forth through the town again — through streets yet more ghost-like in their daylight emptiness than they had seemed yestereven; pattered once more across the wood of the bridge beneath which the sullen waters ran, without appearing to run, as grey and leaden as the heavens above.

And after two hours' dreary tramp along a poplar-bordered, deserted road, we saw before us the gilded iron gateway of Ottilienruhe. Beyond there was a vision of French gardens; of bowling-greens all drenched; of flat terraces whereon the yews, fantastically cut, stood about like the pieces of a chessboard. Beyond that again rose the odd Grecian porticos and colonnades, the Chinese cupolas, appertaining to the summer pleasaunce of the reigning house.

It might have looked fair enough under bright skies in summer weather, with roses on the empty beds and sunshine on the little yellow spires; but it seemed a most desolate place as it lay beneath my eyes that noon. I told myself I should find sunshine enough within, yet my heart lay heavy in my breast.

A sentry, with his pointed fur cap drawn down over his eyes, with the collar of his great-coat drawn up above his ears, so that of his countenance only the end of a red nose was visible to the world, marched up and down before the gates, and, as we made ready to halt, challenged us roughly.

At the sound of his call two more sentries appeared at different points, and tramped towards us with suspicion in their bearing.

Evidently the Duke was well guarded. I rode a few steps forward, when, to my astonishment, it being full peace-time, the fellow brought his musket to the ready, and again cautioned me to pass on my way.

"But my way is to the palace," I bawled to him defiantly, despite the consciousness that the doubtful impression I must myself create could not be mitigated by the sight of János behind me. For I am bound to say that in the plain garb I had insisted on his donning, now much disordered, as I have said, by our travels, with the natural grimness of his countenance enhanced by a screw of pain, a more truculent-looking ruffian it would have been hard to find.

But so far I did not anticipate any more serious difficulty than what a few arguments could remove: and I carried a heavy purse. So I added boldly:

"I have business at the palace."

The man lowered his weapon and came a step nearer.

"Whence come you?" he asked more civilly.

"From Budissin," said I.

The musket instantly went up again, and its bearer retreated hastily a couple of paces.

"'Tis against orders," he said, "because of the sickness; no one from Budissin may pass the gates."

The sickness again! I had, then, by my impetuosity, my haste to follow in her traces, but raised a new barrier between us.

I dismounted, threw my reins to János, and advanced upon the soldier.

"But, friend," said I ——

The fellow covered me with his weapon.

"Stand!" he cried roughly; "stand, or I fire!"

I stood back stock-still. Here was a quandary indeed!

"But, my God!" I cried to him, "I am a traveller. I have but passed through the town. I have come these eighty leagues upon urgent business, and I must see some one who I am told is in the palace."

So saying I drew forth a louis d'or, a stock of which I kept loose for such emergencies in my side pocket, and tossed it to the rascal.

"Now get me speech with a person in authority," said I.

With one hand, and without lowering his firelock, he nimbly caught the coin on the fling and placed it in his mouth, after which he shook his head and remarked indistinctly:

"'Tis no use."

And then at last my sorely-tried patience broke down, impotent otherwise in front of his menacing barrel. I cursed him long and loud with that choiceness and variety of epithet of which my own squadron-life experience as well as my apprenticeship to my great-uncle had given me a command.

The clamour we made first drew the other soldiers, and next a little dapper officer from the guard-room behind the inner gate, who ran out towards us, and at the utmost pitch of his naturally piping voice demanded in the name of all gods, thunders, and lightning-blasts what the matter was.

My particular sentinel's utterance was something impeded by the louis d'or in his cheek, and I was consequently able to offer an explanation before him. Uncovering my head and bowing, I introduced myself in elegant phraseology, though of necessity, for the distance between us, in tones more suited to the parade ground than to a polite ceremony, and laid bare my unfortunate position. I bewailed that through my brief halt in Budissin, ignorant of the infection, I had evidently made myself amenable to quarantine, and requested his courteous assistance in the matter.

My name was evidently quite unfamiliar to his ears, but, perceiving that he had to deal with an equal, the little officer at once returned my salute with an extra flourish, and my civility by ordering the sentry to stand aside. Then, advancing gingerly in the mud to a more reasonable interval for conversation, he informed me, with another sweeping bow, that he was Captain Freiherr von Krappitz, and that, while it would be his pleasure to serve me in every possible manner, he regretted deeply that his orders were such that he could only ratify the sentry's conduct.

"And are there no means, then," cried I, "by which I can communicate in person with any resident of the palace?"

"In person," said the officer, "I regret, none. His Serene Highness's orders are stringent, and when I tell you that our Princess is actually behind these walls, you will understand the necessity. The sickness has been appalling," he added.

He must have seen the blank dismay upon my countenance, for his own sharp visage expressed a comical mixture of sympathy and curiosity, and again approaching two steps he proceeded:

"I could perhaps convey some message. I shall soon be relieved from duty here. The person you wish to see is —— ?"

"It is a lady," said I, flushing.

This was what the little gentleman had evidently expected. Suppressing a grin of satisfaction, he gave another salute and placed himself quite at my disposal. But I had an unsurmountable objection to announce my real relationship to the woman who had fled from my protection. Courteous as my interlocutor was, and honourable and kind as he seemed to be, I could send no message to my wife through him.

"If you will see to the safe delivery of a letter," said I, "I should be grateful indeed."

His face fell.

"It is possible, perhaps," he said dubiously, "but less easy of accomplishment. There will be the necessity of disinfection. If you think your billet-doux — forgive me for supposing you to be a sufferer from the tender passion, and believe me I speak with sympathy" (here he thumped his little chest and heaved from its restricted depths a noisy sigh) — "if you think your billet-doux will not lose of its sweetness by a prolonged immersion in vinegar, I will do what I can. Nay, I think I can promise you that your letter will be delivered, if you will kindly inform me who the fair recipient is to be."

Again I hesitated. I would not call her by her maiden name; to speak of her as my wife, to bawl my strange story on the high road, was not only intolerable to my pride, but seemed inadvisable and certainly imprudent in my ignorance of her attitude at the Court.

"It is," said I, "one of your Princess's Court ladies." And here his volubility spared me further circumlocution.

"It can certainly not be," he cried, "that you have formed an unhappy attachment for the Frau Gräfin von Kornstein? There remains then only the young Comtesse d'Assier, Fräulein von Auerbach and her sister, and Fräulein Ottilie Pahlen — these are all of our fair circle that are now in attendance at the palace."

"It is the last lady," I said, and was at once glad of my own circumspection and troubled in my mind that she should be keeping her secret so well.

"Mes compliments," said he with a smirk, but I thought also with a shade of patronage, as if by mentioning her last he had also shown her to be the last in his worldly esteem. Once, doubtless, this would have galled me.

"Then if I write now," I cried, "and you, according to your kind offer, take charge of my letter, how soon can it be in her hands?"

"But as soon as the guard has relieved me, good sir, am I free to act the gallant Mercury — pity it is that these sordid details of sickness and quarantine should come to spoil so pretty an errand. This was a fair Court for Cupid before the ugly plague came on us. Yes," he added, "I have seen days!"

I had already drawn out my tablets, and, thanking him hurriedly (without, I fear, evincing much interest in his sentimental reflections), turned and, making a standing desk of my horse, with the sheet spread upon the saddle, began, all in the dreary drizzle, to trace with fingers stiffened from the cold the few lines which were to bring my wife back to me.

I had little time for composition, and so wrote the words as they welled up from my heart.

"Dear love," said I, in the French which had been the language of our happiest moments, "your poor scholar has learnt his lesson so well that he cannot live without his teacher. Forget what has come between us. Remember only all that unites us, and forgive. I have, it seems, involved myself in difficulty by passing through Budissin, and so will, I fear, have to endure delay before being permitted sight of your sweet face again. But let me have a word which may help me to bear the separation, let me know that I may carry home my wife." I signed it, "Your poor scholar and loving husband." Then I folded it, fastened it with a wafer, and after a minute's pause decided to burn my ships and address it by the right name of her to whom I destined it — "Madame Ottilie de Jennico, Dame d'honneur de S. A. S. la Princesse Marie Ottilie de Lusace."

Bending over the living desk, — the poor patient brute never budged but for his heaving flanks, — I laid for a second, unperceived I thought, my lips upon that name which haunted me, sleeping and waking, and turning, with the letter in my hand, found the Freiherr watching me, with his head upon one side and so comic an air of sympathy that, at another moment, I should have burst out laughing.

"It is mille dommages," quoth he as, bending his supple spine again, he drew his sword with a charming gesture of courtesy, "that this chaste salute should have to pass through the bitter waves of the Court doctor's vinegar basin before reaching the virginal lips for which it is intended."

"Then I may rely upon your countenance?" said I, unmindful of his mock Versailles floweriness as I fixed my missive to the point of the sword extended towards me for that purpose by the longest arm the little fellow could make. I knew he would not read the tell-tale inscription until the unpoetic process he had so feelingly lamented should have been gone through, and I wondered something anxiously whether it would not prove another complication, my wife in her wounded pride having thus chosen to conceal our marriage — in truth, I might have known it: had she not shaken off my ring? Seeing upon what grounds we had parted, however, I dared not have addressed her otherwise, and so could see no way but to run some risk.

"When may I hope to receive an answer? — you will forgive my impatience," said I, with a somewhat rueful smile, "for you have some knowledge of the human heart, I see, and so I venture further to trespass on your great courtesy. I will meet here any messenger you may depute at any hour you name this afternoon."

"Myself, sir, myself," said the good-natured gentleman, "and in as short a space as possible. Shall we say three o'clock?"

There were then a few minutes wanting to noon by my uncle's famous chronometer. Three hours seemed long, but, as we must ever learn to do in life, I had to be content with a slice where I wanted the loaf. (Now I have not even a crumb for my starving heart, and yet I live.)

As I had surmised, my messenger continued to hold the missive at the extreme length of his weapon and arm, while we made our divers congees and compliments. Thus we parted, he to withdraw to his guard-house, and I, with my attendant, to ride back to the nearest village, with what appetite we might for our noonday meal.

I rode alone again to the rendezvous, full early, poor fool! János I had sent on to find lodgings for me in the neighbourhood, out of range of infection, so that my time of purgatory need not be an hour prolonged.

The sky had cleared somewhat and it rained no more, but there was now a penetrating and moisture-charged wind. A little after the stroke of three my friend of the morning came forth, waved aside the sentry as before, and halted within the former distance, while I dismounted. His countenance was far from bearing the beaming cordiality with which he had last surveyed me, nor had his bow anything like its previous depth and roundness. He drew a folded paper from his pocket, attached it to the point of his sword, according to the process I had already witnessed, and presented it to me, observing drily:

"I regret, sir, that there seems to be some mistake about this matter. The Court doctor, who duly delivered the letter at the palace, informs me that none of her Highness's ladies-in-waiting will consent to receive it, it being indeed addressed to some person unknown among them. There is no lady of the name of Jennico among her Highness's attendants."

I felt myself blanching.

"Am I to understand," said I, "that Fräulein Ottilie Pahlen has repudiated this letter?"

"My good sir," said he, looking at me, I thought, with a sort of compassion, as if he feared I was weak in my head, "I understand from the Court doctor that Mademoiselle Pahlen was the lady to whom the letter was at once offered, according to my request and yours. There is perhaps some mystery?"—here his interest seemed to flicker up again, and he smiled as who would say, "*confide in me*"; but I could not bring my tongue to this humiliation, less than ever then.

I flicked the poor, vinegar-sodden, despised epistle from the point of his sword, and, spreading it out once again, added to it in a sort of frenzy this appeal:

"For God's sake forgive me! You cannot mean to send me away like this. Ottilie, write me one line, for from my soul I love you."

Then I pasted the sheet again, and, drawing a line through the title, wrote above it in great letters:

"Fräulein Ottilie Pahlen," and then I said to the officer:

"You will be doing a deed of truer kindness than you can imagine, Captain von Krappitz, if you will have this letter placed again in the hands of Fräulein Pahlen. More I cannot say now, but some day, if my fortune is not more evil than I dare reflect upon, I will explain."

"Wait here half an hour," he responded with a return of his good nature; "I am off duty and free for the rest of the day. If I can induce the Court doctor to attend to me — in truth, he is of a very surly mood this afternoon — I trust you may see me return a messenger of better tidings."

Besides a very bubbling heat of curiosity there was real amiability in this readiness to help me.

The half hour sped and half an hour beyond it — why do I linger upon such details? From sheer cowardly reluctance, I believe, to describe those moments of my great despair.

And then a cockscomb of a servant fellow, in gorgeous livery and ribboned cue, stepped forth from the gates, sniffing a bunch of stinking herbs, and stood and surveyed me for a second from head to foot, grinning all over his insolent visage, till I wonder how I kept my riding-whip from searing it across.

"Well, sir?" said I sternly.

He felt, maybe, the note of master in my voice, for he cringed a little, and, more civilly than his countenance suggested, requested to know if I was the gentleman with whom Captain the Freiherr von Krappitz had recently been conversing. Upon my reply he gingerly held up a filthy rag of paper, in which I recognised, with a failing of the heart such as I cannot set forth in words, my own letter once more. And in sight of my discomfiture, resuming his native impudence, he proceeded in loud tones:

"My master bids me inform you that he can no longer be the means of annoying a young lady whom he respects so much as Mademoiselle Pahlen. She has requested that your letter may be returned to you again, and declares that she knows no such person as yourself, and is quite at a loss why she should be made the object of this strange persecution."

The rogue sang out the words as one repeating a lesson in which he has been well drilled.

As I stood staring at him, all other feelings swallowed up in the overwhelming tide of my disappointment, I saw him, as in a dream, toss the much-travelled note in the mud between us, turn on his heel, exchange a grin with the nearest sentry, jerk his thumb over his shoulder in my direction, tap his forehead significantly, and finally swagger out of sight behind the little wicket.

And still I stood immovable, unable to formulate a single thought in my paralysed brain, the whole world before me a dull blank, yet knowing that, when I should begin to feel again, it would be hell indeed.

A shout from the sentry suddenly aroused me.

"'Tis better," he called, "that you should move on."

And in good sooth what had I more to do before those gates? I mounted my horse and rode backwards and forwards upon that wretched scrap of paper that had been charged with all the dearest longings of my heart, until it lay indistinguishable in the mud around it. Then I set spurs to my jade, and we rode, a well-matched couple, away towards the strange village where I was to meet János.

With the memory of that bitterest hour of his life burning so hot within him that he could continue his sedentary task no longer, but must rise and pace the room after the sullen way now well known to János as betokening his master's worst moments, Basil Jennico laughed aloud. Pride must have a fall! God knows his pride had had falls enough to kill the most robust of vices.

Had ever man been so humiliated, so contemned as he? Had ever poor soul been made to suffer more relentlessly where it had sinned?

"I have been brought low, very low," said he to himself, and thought of the early days at Tollendhal when its young lord had deemed the whole earth created for his use. Yet, even as he spoke, he knew in his heart that the pride that was born in him would die with him only, and that if it had been mastered awhile it was only but because love had been stronger still.

When he had taken the roturière unreservedly to his heart; when he had returned from the mountains to seek reconciliation; when he had followed her upon her flight, had twice besought her to return to him; when he had made his third and last futile appeal in the face of a slashing rebuff, pride had lain beneath the heel of love. He had been beaten, after all, by a pride greater than his own; and he knew that were she to call him even now, he would come to her bidding in spite of all and through all.

The boards of the narrow, irregular room creaked beneath his impatient tread. Outside, the sounds of traffic were dying away. The last belated coaches had clattered down the streets, the tall running footman had extinguished his link. Basil Jennico turned instinctively towards the south, like the restless compass-needle, a way that had grown into a habit of late as his spirit strove to bridge across the leagues of sea and land that lay between him and his wife.

Was she thinking of him now? What was his curse was at the same time his triumph: he defied her to forget him any more than he could forget her! Those hours, had she not shared them with him? Come what would, no man could lay claim to be to her what he had been. *No man — that way madness lay!* . . .

He looked round at the pages scored with his writings and gave a heart-sick sigh, and then at the door of the room beyond, wherein stood that huge four-post bed where he had tossed through such sleepless hours and dreamed such dreams that the waking moment held the bitterness of death. Next he thought of the town beyond, so full, yet to him so empty.

How to pass the time that went by with such leaden feet? The days were bad enough, but the nights — the nights were terrible! Should he don his most brilliant suit and hie him out into the throng of men of fashion? Some of the Woschutzski gold would not come amiss at the dicing-table of my Lady Brambury, or at the Cocoa-tree, or yet the Hummums, where (his head being as strong as the best of them) he could crack a few bottles in good company. Good company, forsooth! What could all the world be to him for want of that one small being? He might drink himself into oblivion, perhaps, a few hours' oblivion, and be carried home in the early morning and wake at midday with a new headache and the old heartache. Pah!

Of three evils choose the least: since the great feather bed would hold no sleep yet awhile; since to drag his misery into company was to add fire to its fever, Mr. Jennico sat down again to his task, hoping so to weary his brain that it would grant him a few hours' dreamless rest.

CHAPTER II

Captain Basil Jennico's Memoir continued

There is very little more to tell. The new inn wherein I found János established was but a poor place in a poor village, a sort of summer resort abandoned in winter-time save by its own wretched inhabitants. The private chamber allotted to me — it was the only one — was bitter cold, but my choice lay between that and the common room below, full of evil smells and reeking boors and stifling stove heat.

But I was in no mood to reck of bodily inconvenience. My further action had to be determined upon ; and, torn two ways between anger and longing, I passed the evening and the greater part of the night in futile battle with myself.

At length I resolved upon a plan which brought some calm into my soul, and with it a creeping ray of hope.

I would lay my case before the Princess herself. She had been ever kindly in her dealings towards me. I had no reason to imagine but that she was well disposed in my favour; she had had no part in her maid of honour's double dealings with me: I would pray her to speak to the wayward being on my behalf, to place before her her duty towards the husband she had herself chosen.

Thus next morning, as clearly, temperately, and respectfully as might be, I indited my letter, sealed it upon each fold with the Jennico coat-of-arms, and, after deliberation, despatched János with it. The fellow had, according to my orders, purchased fresh horses, and cut a better figure than the yesterday's, when he set off upon his errand. Duly and minutely instructed, he was to present himself at another gate of the palace, and I trusted that, making good use of the purse with which he was supplied, his mission might be more successfully accomplished than had been mine.

And indeed, so far as he was concerned, this was the case. He came back sooner than I had supposed it possible, to inform me that, having been able to say he was not from Budissin, he had been received with civility, and permitted to wait at the guard-house of the north entrance while my letter was carried to the palace. After a short time, the messenger who had taken charge of it had returned, demanded and carefully noted my name, qualities, and exact whereabouts, and bidden him go back to his master with the assurance that the Princess would send her answer.

I waited, tramping the short breadth of my miserable room like a caged wolf, anxiously peering every other minute through the rain-stained window which overlooked the high road.

Reason seemed to offer but one conclusion concerning the result of the last appeal: she would come back to me. My offence — bad as it had been, unmanly towards the woman who had lain in my arms, unworthy of a gentleman towards the lady whom he had resolved to acknowledge as his wife — my offence was not one that so true a penitence might not amply atone for. That was what reason said. But, as often as confidence began to rise in my heart, an instinctive dread overcame it, an unaccountable, ominous misgiving that the happiness I had once held in my hand and so perversely cast from me was never to be mine again. And, as the hours slowly fell away, the dread became more poignant, and the effort to hope more futile.

János had returned with his message about noon. It must have been at least five o'clock (for the world outside was wrapped in murky shadow) when there came a sound on the road that made my heart leap: a clatter of horses' hoofs and the rumbling of a coach. I threw open my window and thrust out my head. How vividly the impression comes back on me now!—the cold rain upon my throbbing temples, the blinding light of joy that filled my brain as I strained my eyes to distinguish in the dusk the nature of the vehicle which announced its approach with such important noise. It was a carriage, guarded by an escort of dragoons, who rode by the door, musket on thigh. An escort! It must be the Princess herself: the Princess come in person, the noble and gentle lady, to bring me back my wife, my love!

Fool! Fool! Fool thrice told! for my vainglorious self-conceit, my loving, yearning heart!

My spirits bounded at one leap to their old important, arrogant level. I threw a hasty glance in the mirror to note that the pallor of my countenance and the disorder of my unpowdered hair were after all not unbecoming. As I dashed along the narrow wooden passage and down the breakneck creaking stairs I will not say that in all the glow of my heart, that had been so cold, there was not now, in this sudden relief from the iron pressure of anxiety, a point of anger against the little truant — a vague determination to establish a certain balance of account, to inflict some mild penance upon her as a set-off against the very bitter one she had imposed on me. A minute ago I would have knelt before her and humbled myself to the very dust: when I reached the door of the drinking-room I was already pluming myself upon a resolution to be merciful.

I broke into the room out of the darkness with my head high, and was at first so dazzled by the light within, as well as by the reeling triumph in my brain, that for an instant I could distinguish nothing.

Then, with a sickening revulsion, with such rage as may have torn the soul of Lucifer struck from the heights of heaven to the depths of hell, I saw the single figure of Captain von Krappitz standing in the middle of the floor with much gravity and importance of demeanour. Flattened against the walls, the boors stood open-mouthed, all struck with amazement; and the little host was bowing anxiously to the belaced officer. Two dragoons guarded the door.

Before even a word was uttered I felt that all was over for me.

Concentrating my energies, then, to face misfortune with as brave a front as I might, I halted before my friend of yesterday, and waited in silence for him to open proceedings.

He bowed to me with great courtesy, looking upon me the while with eyes at once compassionate, curious, and yet respectful, as though upon one of newly-discovered importance, and said:

"I grieve, sir, to be the bearer of an order which may cause you displeasure, but I beg you, being a soldier yourself, to consider me only as the instrument which does not presume to judge but obeys. Be pleased to read this — it is addressed to you."

I took the great sealed envelope with fingers as cold and heavy as marble, broke it open mechanically, and read. At first it was without any comprehension of the words, which were nevertheless set forth in a very free, flowing hand, but presently, as the blood rushed in a tide of sudden anger to my brain, with a quickening and redoubled intensity of intelligence.

"The Princess Marie Ottilie of Sachs-Lausitz," so ran the precious document, "has received M. de Jennico's letter concerning a certain lady.

"M. de Jennico has already been given clearly to understand that his importunities are distressing.

"As the lady in question is a member of the Princess's household, M. de Jennico will not be surprised at the steps which are now taken to secure her against further persecution. He is advised to accept the escort of the officer who carries this letter, and warned that any attempt at resistance, or any future infringement of the order issued by command of his Serene Highness, will be visited in the severest manner."

In a bloody heat of rage I looked up, ready for any folly — to strangle the poor courteous little instrument of a woman's implacable resentment — to find death on the bayonets of the hulking sentinels at the door, and be glad of it, so that I had shed somebody's blood for these insults! But, meeting Captain von Krappitz's steady glance, I paused. And in that pause my sense returned.

If love itself be a madness, as they say, what name shall we give to our wrath against those that we love! For that minute no poor chained Bedlamite could have been more dangerously mad than I. But my British dread of ridicule saved my life that day, and perhaps that of others besides.

Perhaps also the real pity, the sympathy, that was stamped on the captain's honest face had something to say to calming me. At any rate, I recovered from my convulsion, and awoke to the fact that blood was running down my shirt from where I had clenched my teeth upon my lip.

I must have been a fearsome object to behold, and I have a good opinion of Captain von Krappitz's coolness that he should thus have stood and faced a man of twice his size and, in such a frenzy, of probably four times his strength, with never a signal to his guard or even a step in retreat.

Said this gentleman then, delicately averting his

eyes from my countenance, so soon as he saw I had come to my senses:

"If you will glance at this paper you will see that my orders are stringent, and I shall be greatly indebted to your courtesy if you will co-operate in their being carried out in the least unpleasant manner possible. Indeed, sir," he added in my ear hastily and kindly, "resistance would be worse than useless."

I glanced at the paper he presented to me, caught the words: "Order to Captain Freiherr von Krappitz to convey M. de Jennico beyond the frontier of Lusatia, at any point he may himself choose"; caught a further glimpse of such expressions: "formal warning to M. de Jennico never to set foot more within the dominions of the Duke of Lausitz," "severe penalty," and so forth. I glanced, and tossed the paper contemptuously on the table.

That wife of mine had greater interest at the Court than she had been wont to pretend, and she was using it to some purpose. She was mightily determined that her offending husband should pay his debt to her pride, to the last stripe of his punishment.

I smiled in the bitterness of my soul. I was sane enough now, God knows!

Well, she should have her wish, she should be persecuted no longer.

"I place myself entirely at your convenience," said M. de Krappitz discreetly, adding, however, the significant remark, "my order gives me twelve hours."

He picked up the document as he spoke, folded it carefully, and placed it in his breast pocket.

"Oh, as for me," said I, "I ask for no respite." (Could I desire to waste a second before shaking the dust of this cursed country from my feet?) "The time but to warn my servant and bid him truss up my portmanteau and saddle the horses. I understand," I added, with what, I fear, was a withering smile, "that you are kind enough to offer me a seat in your carriage?"

"Ah, my dear sir," returned the little man, with an expression of relief, "what a delightful thing it is to deal with an homme d'esprit!"

And so, in scarce half-an-hour's time, the triumphal procession was ready to set forth. I entered the coach, the Freiherr took his seat behind me, János, impassive, mounted his horse between two dragoons, whilst my own mount was led by a third soldier in the rear. And in this order we set off at a round pace for the Silesian frontier, where I begged to be deposited.

At first my good-tempered and garrulous escort tried in vain to beguile me into some conversation upon such abstract subjects as music and poetry. But his well-meant efforts failed before my hopeless taciturnity, and it was in silence that we concluded the transit between Rothenburg and the border.

As we parted, however, he held out his hand. "Sans rancune, camarade," said he.

What could I do but clasp the good-natured little paw as heartily as I might, and echo, although most untruly, "Sans rancune"? To the very throat I was full of rancour for everything belonging to Lusatia, and I swear the bitterness of it lay a palpable taste on my tongue.

A free man again, I threw myself upon my horse, and took the straightest road for my empty home. János had the wit to speak no word to me, save a direction now and again as to the proper way. And we rode like furies through the cold, wet night.

"Breed a fine stock . . ." had said my good uncle to his heir.

At least, I thought — and the sound of my laugh rang ghastly even in my own ears — if I have brought roture into the family, I am not like now to graft it on the family tree!

CHAPTER III

CAPTAIN BASIL JENNICO'S MEMOIR, RESUMED THREE MONTHS LATER, AT FARRINGDON DANE

SUFFOLK, 14*th April*, 1772.

I HAD thought upon that day when, in my ill temper, I irreparably insulted my wife, that I could never bring myself to face the exposure which a return to England would necessarily bring about. But when I found the desolation and the haunting memories of Tollendhal like to rob me of all I had left of reason and manliness; when, to my restless spirit, the thought of home seemed to promise some chance of diversion and relief, I did not hesitate. Without delay I set to work to put matters at Tollendhal upon a sufficiently regular scale, also to have realised and transferred to my London bankers a sum of money large enough to meet any reasonable demand. This business accomplished, in less than a month from the date of the ill-fated Rothenburg expedition I found myself breathing my native air again.

Before my departure I charged Schultz — and I

know I can rely upon his faithfulness — to be perpetually on the look-out for any communication from Lausitz, and to be ready to give any one immediate cognisance of my whereabouts. It is a forlorn hope.

Although the humour had come upon me to go back to my own land — after the fashion, I fancy, that a sick man deems he will be better anywhere than where he is — and although I did not hesitate to gratify that humour, I was, nevertheless, not blind to the peculiar position I must occupy among my people. I had no desire to lay claim to the honours I had so prematurely announced, no desire to present myself under false colours, even were such an imposture likely to succeed; but neither did I see why I should lay bare to the jeers of the fashionable world, to the sneers of dear relatives and friends, or, more intolerable still, to their compassion, the whole pitiful plot of that comedy which has turned to such tragedy for me. So, when I wrote to my mother to announce my arrival, I adopted a purposely evasive tone.

"It is deeply unfortunate," I wrote, "that you should have broken the bond of secrecy which I enjoined upon you when I informed you of my intended marriage. You know too much of the world, my dear mother, not to understand that when a commoner like myself, however well born and dowered, would contract an alliance with the heiress of a reigning house, it is more than likely that there may be a 'slip 'twixt the cup and the lip.' My cup has been spilt. I come home, a broken-hearted man, to find myself, I fear, owing to your breach of confidence, the laughing-stock of our society. But the yearning for home is too strong upon me to be resisted; I am returning to England at once. If you would not add yet more to the bitterness of my lot you will strenuously deny the report you indiscreetly spread, and warn curiosity-mongers from daring to probe a wound which I could not bear even your hand to touch."

These words, by which I intended to spare myself at least the humiliation of personal explanation, have produced an unexpected effect. My poor mother performed her task so well that I find myself quite as much the hero of the hour over here as if I had brought back my exalted bride.

The mystery in which I am shrouded, the obvious melancholy of my demeanour, the very indifference with which I receive all notice, added, of course, to my wealth, and possibly to the belief that I am still a prize in the matrimonial market, my extraordinary luck at cards, when I can be induced to play, my carelessness to loss or gain — all this has placed me upon a pinnacle which is as gratifying to my mother as (or, so I hear, for I have declined all reconciliation with the renegade) it is galling to my brother and his family.

But the best yet, so far as I am concerned, is that no one has dared to put to me an indiscreet question, and that even my mother, although her wistful eyes implore my confidence, respects my silence.

Now, having tried in vain to find a solace in the pleasures of town, I have betaken myself to that part of the island which is the cradle of our race, to try whether a taste of good old English sport may not revive some interest in my life.

Often in that last month at Tollendhal, when the whole land was locked in ice and the grey sky looked down pitilessly upon the white earth, day by day, with never a change and scarcely a shadow, I thought of the green winters of my youth in the old country; of rousing gallops, with the west wind in my face, across wide fields all verdant still and homely; of honest English faces, English voices, the tongue of the hounds, the blast of the cracked horn, with almost a passion of desire. It seemed to me that, if I could be back in the midst of it all again, I might feel as the boy Basil had felt, and be rid, were it but for the space of a good cross-country run, of that present Basil Jennico whose brain was so weary of working upon the same useless round, whose heart was so sore within him.

So soon therefore as the weather broke — for the winter has been hard even in this milder climate — I accepted my mother's offer of her dower-house, set up a goodly stable of hunters, and established myself at the Manor of Farringdon Dane. I have actually derived some satisfaction from a couple of days' sport, to which a sight of my lord brother's discomfiture, each time I cut him deliberately in the face of the whole field, has added perhaps a grain.

April 29th.

I am this day like the man in the Gospel who, having driven out the devil from his heart and swept and garnished it, finds himself presently possessed of seven devils worse than the first! The demon of wrath I had exorcised, I believed, long ago; the fiend of unrest and longing I had thought these days to have laid too. In spite of her too obdurate resentment, I had no feeling for my wife, wherever she might be, but tenderness. Now, oh, Ottilie, Ottilie! do I most hate thee or love thee? I know not, by my soul! Yet this at least I do know: mine thou art, and mine thou shalt remain, though we never meet again on earth: mine, as I am thine, though the true, good race of Jennico wither and die on my barren stock.

But what serves it to rant in this fashion to myself when I have not even the satisfaction of hearing a contradiction — not even an excuse to shake my fury? Small satisfaction likewise has that puling, mincing messenger to carry back to you, my wife. Poor old man! I am fain to laugh even in my anger when I recall his panic-stricken countenance of an hour ago.

The hounds were to meet at ten this morning at Sir Percy Spalding's, not three miles from here, and so I was taking the day easy. I had but just finished breakfast, and was standing on the steps of the porch quaffing a draught of ale, as I awaited my horse, sniffing the while the moist southern wind; and my thoughts for once were pleasantly occupied — for once the gnawing canker was at rest within me. Presently my attention was awakened by the rumbling sound of wheels; and, looking towards the avenue, yet so sparsely be-leaved as to afford a clear view down its whole length, I saw coming along it, at slow pace, a heavy vehicle, which in time disclosed itself as a shabby, hired travelling chaise, drawn by an ancient horse, and driven by that drunken scoundrel Bateman from Yarmouth, once a familiar figure to my childish eyes. My heart leaped. I expected no one — my mother was at Cheltenham for the waters —

no one, save, indeed, her whom I ever unconsciously await!

It was perhaps the unreasonable disappointment that fell upon me, when, gazing eagerly for a glimpse of the occupant, as the carriage lumbered through the inner gate, I saw that it contained but the single figure of an old man (huddled, despite the spring warmth of the day, in furs to the very chin) that turned me into so bitter and black a temper.

Even as the chaise drove up before the steps, and as I stood staring down at it, motionless, although within me there was turmoil enough, the fellows came round with my horses. Bess, the Irish mare, took umbrage at the little grotesque figure that, with an alertness one would scarcely have given it credit for, skipped from the chaise, looking more like one of those images I have seen on Saxon clocks than anything human. How she plunged and how the fool that held her stared, and how I cursed him for not minding his business — it was a vast relief to my feelings — and how the old gentleman regarded us as one newly come among savages, and how he finally advanced upon me mincing — I laugh again to think back upon it! But I had no mind to laughter then. 'Twas plain, before he opened his mouth to speak, that my visitor hailed from foreign parts. And at closer acquaintance the reason why, even from a distance, he had appeared to me as something less than human, became evident. His countenance was shrivelled and seared by recent smallpox; scarred in a manner perfectly fantastic to behold.

That curse of my life, that persistent hope — I believe I could get along well enough, but 'tis the hope that kills me — began to stir within me.

"Have I the honour of speaking to Captain Basil de Jennico?" said the puppet in French; and before the question was well out of his mouth, I had capped it with another, breathless:

"Come you not from Rothenburg?"

He bowed and scraped: each saw he had his answer. I was all civility now, Heaven help me! and cordial enough to make up for a more discourteous reception.

I ordered my horses back to the stables, dismissed the chaise, in spite of the newcomer's protestations, and led him within the house, calling for refreshments for him; all the while a thousand questions, to which I yet dreaded the answers, burning on my tongue.

I had installed him in the deepest armchair in the apartment I habitually used; I had kindled a fire with my own hands, for he was shivering in his furs, whether from fear, embarrassment, or cold, I know not — maybe all three together; I had placed a glass of wine at his elbow, which he sipped nervously when I pressed him; and then, when I knew that I should hear what had brought him, from very cowardliness I was mute. It seemed to me as if my courtesies embarrassed him, and that this augured ill, although (I reasoned with myself) if she should send me a messenger at all, I ought to anticipate good tidings.

"I am fortunate, sir," began the old man in quavering tones, "to find you at home. Sir, I have come a long way to seek you. I went first to your castle at Tollendhal, where your steward, a countryman of my own, to whose politeness I am much indebted, gave me very careful instructions as to the road to your English domicile. A most worthy and amiable person! I should not so soon have had the advantage of making your acquaintance had it not been for the help he gave me. I have come by Yarmouth, sir: the wind was all in our favour. I am informed we had a good passage." Here he shivered, and a yet greener shade underspread the scars upon his brow. "But I am not accustomed to the sea, and I have been ill, sir, lately, very ill."

He coughed awkwardly, reached out his trembling hand for the wine, but put down the glass again untasted.

"Surely I am right in believing," said I, "that you come from some one very dear to me — from one from whom I am parted by a series of unfortunate misunderstandings?" I felt my lips grow cold as I spoke, and I know that I panted.

"If you have a letter," said I, "give it to me."

I reached out my hand, and saw, with a strange sort of self-pity, that it shook no less than had the old man's withered claw.

"Or if you have a message," cried I, breaking out at last, "speak, for God's sake!"

He drew back from my impetuosity. There was fear of me in his eye; at the same time, I thought, with a chill about my heart, compassion.

"My good sir," he said, between "hums" and "ha's" which well-nigh drove me distracted, "I believe I may say — in fact, I will venture to assert that I have come from the — ahem, ahem! — young lady I apprehend you speak of. I have been made aware of the — ah, hum! — unfortunate circumstances. The young lady ——." Here he hitched himself up in his chair and began to fumble in the skirts of his floating coat. Between his furs and his feebleness this was a sufficiently lengthy operation to give time for my hopes to kindle stronger again and my small stock of patience to fail.

"You are doubtless prepared to hear," he went on at length, "that the young lady, being now fully alive to the consequence of her — her — ill-considered conduct — a girlish freak, sir, a child's, I may say! — believes that she will be meeting your wishes, nay, your express desire, by joining with you in an application to his Holiness for the immediate annulment of so irregular a marriage."

"What?" cried I with a roar, leaping from my chair. So occupied had I been in watching the movements of his hands as he fingered a great pocket-book, expecting him every instant to produce a letter from her to me, that I had scarce heeded the drift of his babble till the last words struck upon my ear.

"Annul our marriage!" I thundered, "at my desire! In the devil's name, who are you, and whence come you, for it could not be my wife who has sent you with such a message to me?"

The little man had jumped, too, at my violence — like a grasshopper. But my question evidently touched his pride in a sensitive quarter, and roused him to a sense of offence in which he forgot his tremors.

"Truly, sir, truly, you remind me," he said

tartly. "If you will have but a little patience, I was in the very act of seeking my credentials when you so — ahem! — impetuously interrupted me."

As he spoke, with a skip and a bow, which recalled I know not what vague memory of a bygone merry hour, he drew forth a folded sheet, and, unfolding it, presented it to me. I knew the handwriting too well to doubt its authenticity. How often had I conned and kissed the few poor lines she had ever written to me; ay, although they had been penned in her assumed character!

"To M. DE JENNICO —
"I empower M. de Schreckendorf to act for me in the affair M. de Jennico wots of, and I agree beforehand to all his arrangements.

(Thereto the signature.)

Not a word more; not a word of regret, even of anger! The same implacable, unbending resentment.

I stood staring at the lines, reading them and re-reading them, and each letter seemed to print itself like fire upon my soul. I heard, as in a dream, my visitor pour forth further explanations, still in that tone of injury my roughness had evoked.

"I am myself, sir, a friend. Yes, I may say a friend, an old friend, of the young lady. Her parents—ahem!—have always reposed confidence in me. I, sir, am M. de Schreckendorf. The very fact, I should think, of my being in possession of this letter, of this document"—here there was a great rattling of stiff parchment—"will assure you, I should hope, of my identity. Nevertheless, if you wish further proof, I have a letter to our ambassador in London, and I am willing to accompany you to his house, or meet you there at your convenience. Indeed, it would perhaps be more proper and correct, in every way, that the whole matter should be settled and the documents duly attested at the residence of the accredited representative of Lusatia. I will not disguise to you that his Serene Highness, the Duke himself, takes — takes an interest in the lady, and is desirous of having this business, which so nearly affects the welfare and credit of a well-known member of his Court, settled in the promptest and most efficacious manner. A sad escapade, you must admit yourself!"

And all the while my heart was crying out within me in an agony, "Oh, Ottilie, how could you, how could you? Was the memory of those days nothing to you? Is the knowledge of my love and sorrow nothing to you? Are you a woman, and have you no forgiveness?"

Taking perhaps my silence for acquiescence (for this messenger of my wife, albeit entrusted with so delicate a mission, was no shrewd diplomatist), M. de Schreckendorf here spread out with an agreeable flourish an amazing-looking Latin document with rubrics ready filled up, it seemed, but for certain spaces left blank, for the names, I suppose, of the appealing parties.

"I have been led to understand," pursued he then in tones of greatly increased confidence, "that you entirely concur in the lady's desire for the annulment of this contestable union, the actual legality of which, indeed, is too doubtful to be worth discussing. From the religious point of view, however, one of chief importance to my young friend (I think I may call her so), the matter is otherwise serious, for there was, no doubt, a sacrament administered by a priest, duly ordained, but unfortunately, through old age and natural infirmity, wanting in due prudence, and further misled as to the identity of one of the contracting persons. A sacrament, sir, there undoubtedly was; but I am glad to inform you that special leading divines have been already approached upon the subject, and they give good hope, sir, good hope, that a properly drawn up petition, supported by the signatures of the two persons concerned, will meet at Rome with most favourable consideration. The ecclesiastical part of the difficulty once settled, the legal one goes of itself."

I was gradually becoming attentive to the run of his glib speech. I hardly know now how I contained myself so far, but I kept a rigid silence, and for yet another minute or two gave him all my ear.

"Such being the case," he continued, "I need hardly trouble you to disturb yourself by journeying all the way to London. We need proceed no farther than Yarmouth, indeed, and there in the presence of two competent witnesses — I would suggest a priest of our religion and some neighbouring gentleman of substance — all you will have to do is just to sign this document. I repeat, I understand that you are naturally anxious likewise to be delivered from a marriage in which you have considered yourself aggrieved: and not unnaturally." Here the little monster threw a sly look at me, and added: "You were made the victim of a little deception, eh? Then in the course of a few months — Rome is always slow, you know — you will both be as free as air! With no more loss to either of you than the loss of—ahem!—a little inexperience."

As free as air! *Ottilie as free as air!* Then it was that the violence of my wrath overflowed. That moment is a blank to my memory. I only know that I heard the sound of my own voice ringing with shattering violence in the room, and I came to myself again to find that, with a strength my fury alone could have lent, I was shredding the tough parchment between my fingers, so that the ground was strewn with its rags. What most restored me to something like composure was the abject terror of the unlucky messenger, who, huddled away from me in a corner of the room, was peeping round a chair at me, much as you might see a monkey caught in mischief. His teeth were chattering! Good anger was wasted on so miserable an object, and indeed the feelings that swayed me had had roots in ground such as he could never tread upon.

"Come out, M. de Schreckendorf," I said, with a calmness which surprised myself — but there are times when a man's courage rises with the very magnitude of a calamity — "you have nothing to fear from me. You will want an answer to carry back to her that sent you. Take her this."

I stooped as I spoke, and gathered together the

shreds of the document, folded them in a great sheet of paper, and tied it with ribbon into a neat parcel.

"Not a word," I went on; "I will hear no more! When you have rested and partaken of refreshment, one of my carriages will be at your disposal for whatever point you may desire to reach to-day. Stay, you will want some evidence to show that you have fulfilled your embassy."

Sitting down to my writing-table, I hastily addressed the packet to "Madame Basil de Jennico," adding thereafter her distinctive title as maid of honour. This done, I sealed it with my great seal, M. de Schreckendorf meanwhile uttering uncouth little groans.

"Here, sir," said I, holding out the packet with its bold inscription, "they will no longer, it is evident, deny the existence at the Court of Lusatia of the person I have here addressed. Here, sir. Take this to my wife, and tell her that her husband has more respect than she has for the holy sacrament he received with her. Here, sir!"

At every "Here, sir," I advanced a step upon him, holding out the bundle, and at every step I took he retreated, till impatiently I flung it on the table nearest him, and making him a low ironical bow of farewell, turned to leave him.

I paused a moment on the threshold of the

room, however, and had the satisfaction of seeing him, after throwing his hands heavenwards, as if in despairing protest, bring them down again on the packet and proceed to stuff it into the recesses of his coat.

I turned once more to go, when to my surprise he called after me in tones unexpectedly stern and loud:

"Young man, young man, this is a grave mistake; have a care!"

I shrugged my shoulders and slammed the door upon his warning cry. Nor, though he subsequently sent twice by my servants — first to demand, then to supplicate, a further interview — would I consent to parley with him again.

I passed a couple of restless hours, until, at length, from an upper window I saw him depart from my house in far greater state and comfort than he had come.

Now, as I write, I know that he is being whirled along the Yarmouth road at the best pace of my fine horses, speeding back to Lausitz to take my wife my eloquent answer.

CHAPTER IV

NARRATIVE OF AN EPISODE AT WHITE'S CLUB, IN WHICH CAPTAIN JENNICO WAS CONCERNED, SET FORTH FROM CONTEMPORARY ACCOUNTS

THE tenth hour of an October night had rung out over a fog-swathed London; yet, despite the time of year, unfashionable for town life, despite the unpropitious weather, the long card-room at White's was rapidly filling. The tables, each lit by its own set of candles, shone dimly like a little green archipelago in a sea of mist. Groups were gathering round sundry of these boards; the dice had begun to rattle, voices to ring out. The nightly scene was being repeated, wherein all were actors, down to the waiters, who had their private bets, and lost and won with their patrons.

Somewhat apart in the seclusion of a window-recess, cosily ensconced so as to profit of the warmth of the great yellow fire, sat three gentlemen. A fourth chair remained vacant at their table; and from the impatient glances which two of the party now and again turned upon the different doors, it was evident that the arrival of its expected occupant was overdue. The third gentleman, who bore the stamp of a distinctly foreign race, — although his hair, which he wore but slightly powdered, was of a fair hue, and his face rather sanguine than dark, — seemed to endure the delay with complete indifference. His attention was wholly given to the shuffling of a pack of cards, which he manipulated with extreme dexterity, while he listened to his companions' remarks with impassive countenance. He was a handsome man, despite a bulk of frame and feature which almost amounted to coarseness; hardly yet in the prime of life, with full blue eyes and full red lips, which took, when he spoke or smiled, a curious curve, baring the canine in almost sinister fashion. The Chevalier de Ville-Rouge, introduced at White's by the Prussian Ambassador, as a distinguished officer of the great Frederick visiting England for his pleasure, had shown himself so daring a player as to be welcomed among the most noted gamblers. He had lost and won large sums with great breeding, and had in his six weeks' stay contrived to improve an imperfect knowledge of an alien tongue in such fashion as to make intercourse with his English companions quite sufficiently easy.

The youngest of the trio at the table in the

corner, this foggy night, was naturally the one to display his feelings most openly. A clean-faced, square-built English lad, fresh it would seem from the playing fields of school, yet master of his title and fortune, and cornet in the Life Guards, Sir John Beddoes was already a familiar figure in the club, as indeed his finances could bear doleful testimony. The green cuff-guards adjusted over his delicate ruffles, the tablets and pencil ready at his elbow, it was clear he was itching to put another slice of his patrimony to the hazard. His opposite neighbour, Beau Carew (as he dearly loved to hear himself dubbed), was a man of another kidney, and fifteen years of nights, systematically turned into days, had left their stamp upon features once noted for their beauty. Though ready now with a sneer or jest for his companion's youthful eagerness, his eyes wandering restlessly from the clock to the doors betrayed an almost equal anxiety to begin the business of the evening.

"Devil take Jennico!" cried the Baronet at last, striking the table so that the dice leaped in their box; "'pon my soul it's too bad! He gave me an appointment here at ten to-night, and it wants now but six minutes to eleven."

"Bet he comes before the clock strikes," interposed Mr. Carew; "ten guineas?"

"Done with you, Dick," said Sir John promptly.

The bet was registered, and five minutes passed in watching the timepiece on the mantel-shelf: all the young Baronet's eagerness being now against the event he had been burning to hasten. The strokes rang out. With a smile he held out his broad palm, into which Carew duly dropped ten pieces.

"'Tis the first bit of luck the fellow has brought me yet. Gad, I believe my luck has turned! Why the devil don't he come, that I may ease him of a little of that superfluous wealth of his? I swear he gets more swollen day by day, while we grow lean — eh, Carew? — like the kine in the Bible. D—— him!"

"The water goes to the river, as the French say, in spite of all our dams," sniggered Carew; "but as for me I am content that you should go on playing with Jennico so that I may back him; my purse has not been in such good condition for many a long day. Poor devil! How monstrous unfortunate his amours must still be! I only wish," with a conscious wriggle, "he could give me the recipe."

"Yet you have lost on him now," retorted Beddoes, tapping his breast pocket, "and if you back him to-night, you lose on him again, I warn you. I am in the vein, I tell ye! But there is the quarter! Rot him, I believe he is going to rat after all! Bet you he don't come till half-past, Carew. Fifty?"

"Done," said Carew quietly, noting down the entry. "He *is* erratic, I grant you — he, he, he! — did you note me, Chevalier? But he has a taste for the table, though I believe he'd as soon lose as win, were it only for the sake of change. 'Tis about all he cares for — the dullest dog! Bet you there is not a man in the room has heard him laugh."

"You won't find any fool to take up that bet, Carew. Heigh-ho! I'd willingly accommodate myself with a little of his melancholy at the price."

"Better look up a princess for yourself then, Jack," said Carew; "perhaps the Chevalier here can give you an introduction to some other fascinating German Highness."

"Won't it do over here?" asked Beddoes, with a grin. "D'ye think I'd have a chance with Augusta? Twenty past! Let him keep away till the half-hour now. Zounds! 'twould be a mean trick if he failed me on my lucky night; though I don't want him for ten minutes yet. He has fairly cleared me out; the team will have to go next if I don't get back some of my I O U's."

"Why, it would be a very good thing for thee, Jack, if he played thee false. I say so though I should lose most damnably by it. Thy team will go, thy coaches will go, thy carts, thy grooms, thy dog, thy cat. Why, man, thou must lose — 'tis as plain as the nose on Lady Maria's face. And he must win, poor wretch, and I too, since I back him. Ask the Chevalier if it is not a text of truth all the world over: lucky at cards, unlucky in love. Never look so sulky, boy; 'tis providential compensation."

"You surprise me, gentlemen," said the Chevalier, with a strong guttural accent, lifting as he spoke his heavy lids for the first time. "I was not aware that Captain Jennico was so afflicted in his affections."

"You surprise *me*, Chevalier," returned Carew gaily. "I deemed you and he such friends. Why, I won a hundred from my Lord Ullswater but yestereven by wagering him that you would be the only man in the room to whom Jennico would speak more than ten words within the hour. The counting was not difficult. He said sixty-four to you and five to Jack."

"Mr. Jennico has certainly shown me both kindness and sympathy," said the Chevalier, who had now folded his strong white hands over the pack of cards, and sat the very embodiment of repose. "Doubtless our having both served in the same part of the world, though under different standards, has somewhat drawn us together: but he has not made me his confidant."

"And so you don't know the tale of Jennico and the Princess? 'Tis a dashed fine tale. Carew, you are a wit, or think you are — it comes to much the same thing: tune up, man, give your version; for," turning to the Chevalier again, "there are now as many versions current as days in the month. 'Tis twenty-five minutes past; you had better get your I O U ready, Master Carew."

"I have three hundred chances yet," said Carew. Then turning to the foreigner, "Would you really, sir, care to hear the true story of our friend's discomfiture? I am about the only man in town that knows the *true* one; but all that's old scandal now — town talk of last year, as stale as Lady Villiers's nine virgin daughters. There are a dozen new ones since. Would you not rather hear the last of his Royal Highness the Duke of C. and Lady W.? That is choice if you like, and as fresh as Rosalinda's last admirer — eh, John?"

"I am not fond," said the Chevalier drily, "of hearing those discussed who, being High Born, have the right to claim respect and homage. But I confess to some interest in my friend Mr. Jennico."

"Begad, then," responded Mr. Carew, flicking a grain of snuff from the ruffles of his pouting bosom, "I cannot promise to spare your scruples concerning scandal in high quarters, for the heroine of the romance is, it would appear, one of your own German royalties; but since you wish the story, you shall have it. There is then a certain Dorothea Maria Augusta Carolina Sophia, etc., etc., daughter of some Duke of Alsatia, Swabia, Dalmatia — no, stay, Lusatia, wherever that may be; ay, that's the name — one of your two hundred odd principalities — you know all about it, I don't — and Jennico, who, as you are aware, was in the Imperial service, met this wondrously beautiful Princess at some Court function somewhere. They danced, they conversed, she was fair and he was fond — fill it in for yourself. He thought himself a tremendous cock of the walk; to be brief, he aspired to act King Cophetua and the beggar maid, turned the other way, with the exception that he is as rich as Crœsus. He made so sure of the lady's favour that he wrote over to his mother to announce the marriage as a settled thing. A royal alliance, with the prospect of speedily mounting to the throne on the strength of his wife's pretensions! Ha, ha!"

"'Tis a droll story," said the Chevalier gravely; "and then?"

"Oh, then!— Zounds! you can conceive the flutter in the dovecot over him. My Lady Jennico, his mother, was blown out with pride, swimming in the higher regions, a perfect balloon! Gad, she would no longer bow to any one less than a Duke! She ran hither and thither cackling the news like the hen that has laid an egg. She sent — I was told on the best authority — to the Lord Chamberlain to know what precedence the young couple would be given at the next Birthday. She called at the College of Arms to inquire about the exact marshalling of the coat of Lusatia with that of Jennico. He, he! And whether the resultant monstrosity would comport a royal crown!"

"Faith, that's a good one," said Sir John, with a guffaw; "I had not heard *that*, Carew."

"Fact, fact, I assure you," smiled the wit.

"Very droll," repeated M. de Ville-Rouge, with impassive muscles.

"When," continued Carew, "lo and behold, what a falling off was there, as young Roscius says! What a come down! Humpty-Dumpty was nothing to it — poor Lady Jennico's egg!

Ah! well, we all know pride must have a fall. Your fair compatriot, sir, had but amused herself with the fine Englishman, for which I would be loath to blame her. She gave him, it is said, indeed, every pledge of her affection. But when he began to prate of rings and marriage lines, and pressed her to become Mrs. Jennico, she found him a little too presumptuous — at least, I take it so; and being, it would seem, of a merry turn of mind, devised a little joke to play upon him. Pretending to yield at last to his urgency, she gave her consent to a secret marriage, and in the dark chapel palmed off her chambermaid upon him! Ha, ha! So the poor devil, carrying off his bride by night in high glee, thinking himself a very fine fellow indeed, never discovered till he had brought her home that he had given his hand and name to a squinting, sausage-nosed, carroty maid, daughter of the Court confectioner, called in baptism by the Princess's names, like half the girls in the town. The story goes that the Princess with all the Court were waiting at his house to see the happy pair arrive, and I have had secret, but absolutely incontestable, information that the Princess laughed till she had to be bled."

M. de Ville-Rouge smiled at last in evident appreciation of the humour of the situation.

"It is, on my honour, a most comic story," he said. "But how come you so well acquainted with the matter? Surely my poor friend Jennico has ill-chosen his confidant."

"Devil a word have I heard from Jennico," said Carew. "Faith, he has ever been the same cheerful, conversational fellow you wot of, and it would take a bold man to question him. But truth, you know, will out — truth will out in time."

"Ay," said the Chevalier, and was shaken with silent merriment.

"Half-past eleven," roared the Baronet, suddenly, stretching out a great paw and snapping his fingers under the beau's face.

"Zounds!" cried the wit, turning to look at the clock with some discomposure; "no, Jack, no, there is still a fraction of a minute — the half-hour has not struck. And, by Heaven, here's our man! Had you not better sup with Rosalinda to-night?"

Sir John, in the act of looking round pettishly — he had not yet reached that enviable state of mind in which a gambler declares that the greatest delight after winning is that of losing — found his attention unexpectedly arrested by the countenance of the Chevalier de Ville-Rouge, which presented at that moment such an extraordinary appearance that the young man forgot his irritation, and remained gazing at it in open-mouthed astonishment.

The features, usually remarkable for their set, rather heavy composure, were perturbed to the verge of distortion. The whole face was stained with angry purple, the veins of the forehead swollen like whipcord.

Sir John Beddoes's wits were none of the sharpest, but it was clear even to him that the emotion thus expressed was one of furious disappointment.

But while he cudgelled his brains for an explanation of this sudden humour in a man who was neither winner nor loser by Basil Jennico's appearance, the face of the Chevalier resumed its wonted indifferent expression and dulness of hue with a rapidity that altogether confounded the observer.

By this time the tall figure of the new-comer had wended its way down the room and was close upon them. All turned to greet him, and poor Sir John found his feelings once more subjected to a shock.

The acquaintances of Basil Jennico were accustomed to find his brow charged with gloom, to see his cheek wear the pallor of one who sleeps little and thinks much. But in his demeanour to-night was more than the usual sombreness, on his countenance other than natural pallor. As he stood for a moment responding absently to the Chevalier's hearty greeting, and Carew's bantering salutation of "All hail!" it became further apparent that his dress was disordered, that his ruffles were torn and blood-stained, that his brocade jacket was jaggedly rent upon the left side, and also ominously stained here and there.

"Gadzooks, man!" exclaimed Carew, his bleared grey eyes lighting at the prospect of a new wholesale scandal for his little retail shop. "What has happened thee? Wounded? How? Ah, best not inquire perhaps! Beddoes, lad, see you he has got reasons for his delay. Who knows but that you may have a chance to-night after all. A deadly dig, well aimed under the fifth rib, a true Benedick's pinking; or shall we say goring?— ahem! Have a care, Jennico, these wounds from horned beasts are reputed ill to heal. Ah, sad dog, sad dog! I will warrant thou hast had the balance nevertheless to thy credit. Now do I remember a little lady was casting very curious looks at you at Almack's last night."

Basil had flung himself into the chair that had so long awaited him, and seemed to lend but a half-apprehending ear to the prattler on his left, who, as he leant towards him, was hardly able to restrain his eager hand from fingering the hurt so unmistakably evidenced. On the right the Chevalier as unsuccessfully pressed him with earnest queries, manifesting, it would seem, a genuine anxiety.

"Great God, my friend! what has happened?"

The stentorian tones of Sir John Beddoes, who saw an opportunity of retrieving his fortunes, here broke in hastily upon Carew's flow of words: "Bet you double or quits it was *not* Lady Sue," and aroused Mr. Jennico's attention.

"I should be loath to spoil sport," he said, "but I advise no one to bet on my bonnes fortunes. This scratch — for it is nothing more, Mr. Carew, and I would show it to you with pleasure in reward for your flattering interest, but the surgeon has just bound it up very neatly, and it would be a pity to disturb his handiwork — is but the sixth of a series of attempts on my life, made within the last six weeks, by persons unknown, for purposes likewise unknown."

"Dash it, Jennico, you might have let me enter the bet," said the Baronet sulkily, while Carew, sniffing a choicer titbit of gossip than he had expected, wriggled with pleasure, and the Chevalier expressed unbounded amazement that such a state of things could exist, above all in England.

"It is even so," resumed Basil, turning to the last speaker as if glad to give vent to some of his pent-up irritation. "I confess that when I returned to my native land I did expect to find at least a quiet life. Why, in my house at Tollendhal, where those who surrounded me were half savages, ruled by the stick and the halter, where it was deemed imprudent for the master to walk the roads without his body-guard, there was never so much as a stone thrown after me. But here, in old England, my life, I believe, would not be worth backing for a week." He looked round with a smile in which melancholy and disdain were blended.

"Now, d—— me!" cried Sir John, struck in his easy good nature into sudden warmth and sympathy, "nay, now d—— me, Jennico! I will take any man a hundred guineas that you are alive this day month."

"Done!" said the Chevalier, with such unexpected energy that all three turned round to look at him with surprise; perceiving which he went on, laughing to conceal an evident embarrassment: "Your betting habits here are infectious, but while I will not withdraw, I am prepared to be glad to lose rather than gain for once." He fixed Basil across the table with his brooding eye as he spoke, and bowed to him, then turned to the Baronet. "No, Sir Beddoes, I am not going to recede from the wager."

This, as a wager worth recording, was forthwith entered into the club book. Basil looked on, half in amusement, half in bitterness.

"'Tis likely, after all," he said, addressing Sir John, "that you may win and that the Chevalier may be afforded the pleasure of losing, for I seem to bear a charmed life. Perhaps," he added with a sigh, "because I care so little for it. Though to be sure there is something galling to a man in being shot at from behind a hedge and set on in the dark; in not knowing where the murderer may be lying in wait for him, at what street corner, at what turn of the road, behind what hayrick. If I have not kept my appointment over punctually to-night, it is because a rogue has had me by the Park gateway in Piccadilly. There is more here than mere accidental villainy. The next will be that I shall see murder in my own servant's eyes. Or, who knows, find it lying at the bottom of my cup. Pah! I am as bold as most men; I would welcome death more readily than most; but, by Heaven! it is unfair treatment, and I have had more than my share of it."

"Why, Jennico," said Carew, "you never spoke

a word of this before. A fellow has no right to keep such doings dark. Tell us the details."

"Ay, tell us all about it," said Sir John, with round eyes ready to start from their orbits.

"True," said Basil, "you have now an interest, Jack, in knowing what sort of odds are against you. Well, you shall learn all you wish; but let us to supper, gentlemen, meanwhile, that we may lose no further time and start better fortified upon the evening's business, if Beddoes is still anxious for his revenge."

CHAPTER V

Narrative of an Episode at White's continued

It was over a dish of devilled kidneys and a couple of bottles of Burgundy that — pressed by the eager curiosity of his English friends, no less than by the interest M. de Ville-Rouge continued to profess in his concerns with all Teutonic earnestness — Basil Jennico began to narrate his misadventures in the same tone of ironical resentment with which he had already alluded to them.

"It began at Farringdon Dane," he said, "on the little property in Suffolk which my mother has placed at my disposal. 'Twas some six weeks gone, walking through the wood at sundown, I was shot at from behind a tree. The charge passed within an inch of my face, to embed itself in a sapling behind me. I was, according to my wont — an evil habit — deeply absorbed in thought, and was alone; consequently, although I searched the copse from end to end, I could find no trace of my well-wisher. That was number one. I gave very little heed to the occurrence at first, believing it to be some poacher's trick, or maybe the unwitting act of what you call in your country, Chevalier, a Sunday sportsman, who mistook my brown beaver for the hide of a nobler quarry. But the next attempt gave me more serious food for reflection. This time I was shot at while sitting reading in my study at night, when all the household had retired. It was close weather, and I had drawn the curtains and opened the windows. The bullet again whizzed by my ear, and this time shattered the lamp beside me. No doubt the total darkness which ensued saved me from a second and better aim."

"You are a fortunate young man," said the Chevalier gravely.

"Do you think so, Chevalier?" answered Jennico, with a smile which all the bitterness of his thoughts could not altogether rob of sweetness. "I do not think any one need envy my fate. Well, gentlemen, you can conceive the uproar which ensued upon the event I have just described. The best efforts of myself, my servants, and my dogs failed, however, to track the fugitive, although the marks of what seemed a very neat pair of shoes were imprinted on my mother's most choice flower-beds. After this adventure I received a couple more of such tokens of good-will in the country.

Once I was shot at crossing a ford in full daylight, and my poor nag was struck; this time I did catch a glimpse of the scoundrel, but he was mounted too, and poor Bess, though she did her utmost, fell dead after the first twenty strides in pursuit. Thereupon my mother grew so morbidly nervous, and the mystery resisting all our attempts at elucidation, I gave way to her entreaties and returned to London, where she deemed I would find myself in greater safety."

"And has your friend followed you up here?" exclaimed Sir John, forgetting his supper in his interest. "By George, this is a good story!"

"I was stopped on the road by a highwayman," answered Mr. Jennico quietly. "Nothing unusual in that, you will say; but there was something a little out of the common nevertheless in the fact that he fired his pistol at me without the formality of bidding me stand and deliver; which formality, I believe, is according to the etiquette of the road. I am glad to tell you that I think we left our mark on the gentleman this time, for as he rode away he bent over his saddle, we thought, like one who will not ride very far. But, faith! the brood is not extirpated, and the worthy folk who display such an interest in me, finding hot lead so unsuccessful, have now taken to cold steel."

Sir John Beddoes damned his immortal soul with great fervour.

"Pray, sir," remarked Mr. Carew with an insinuating smile, "may not the identity of the murderer be of easier solution than you deem? Are there no heirs to your money?"

"I might pretend to misunderstand you, Mr. Carew," said Basil, flushing, "although your meaning is plain. Permit me to say, however, that I fail to find a point to the jest."

"'Twas hardly likely you would find humour in a point so inconveniently aimed against yourself," answered Carew airily. "But 'tis a rarity, Jennico, to find a man ready to take up the cudgels for his heirs and successors. Nevertheless, I crave your pardon, the more so because I am fain to know what befell you to-night."

"To-night was an ill night to choose for so evil an attempt," said the Chevalier, rousing himself from a fit of musing and looking reflectively round upon the fog, which hung ever closer even in the warm and well-lit room.

"It was the very night for their purpose, my dear Chevalier," returned the young man with artificial gaiety. "Faith, it was like to have succeeded with them, and I make sure mine enemy, whoever he may be, is pluming himself even now upon the world well rid of my cumbersome existence. I was on foot, too, and what with the darkness and emptiness of the streets I was, I may say, delivered into their hands. But they are sad bunglers. One of my pretty fellows in Moravia would have done such a job for me, were I in the way to require it, as cleanly and with as little ado as you pick your first pheasant in October, Jack. And yet it may be that I am providentially preserved — preserved for a better fate." Here he tossed off his glass as if to a silent toast.

"But why on foot, my dear Jennico? On foot — fie, fie, and in this weather! What could you expect?" cried Carew with a shiver of horror.

"If you were not so fond of interruption, Mr. Carew," said the Chevalier with a sinister smile, "perhaps we might sooner get to the end of Mr. Jennico's story. We are all eagerness to hear about this last miraculous preservation."

"I hardly know myself how I come to be alive! I could get no sedan, my dear Carew, and that was just the rub. What with Lady Bedford's card-party and the fog, there was not one to be had within a mile, and I had given my stablemen a holiday. I sent my servant upon the quest for a chair, but got tired of waiting, mindful of my appointment with my friend and neighbour here, and so it was that I set forth, as I said, on foot and alone. The mist was none so thick but that I could find my way, and I was pursuing it at a round pace when, opposite Devonshire House, some fellow bearing a link crossed from over the road, came straight upon me without a word, raised his torch, and peered intently into my face. I halted, but before I could demand the meaning of his insolence down went his fire-brand fizzing into the mud, out came his sword, and I was struck with such extreme violence that, in the very attempt to recover my balance, I fell backwards all my length upon the pavement, skewered like a chicken, and carrying the skewer with me. Some gentlemen happened to reach the spot at that moment, there was a cry for the watch, but the rogue had made good use of his heels and the fog, and was out of sight and hearing in a moment."

"Verdammt villain!" cried M. de Ville-Rouge, whose brow had grown ever blacker during this account. "Say, my amiable friend, did you not get even a lunge at him?"

"Lunge, man! I was skewered, I tell you; I could not even draw! His sword — 'twas as sharp as a razor, a fine sword, I have had it brought to my chambers — had gone clean through innumerable folds of cloak and cape, back and front, only to graze my ribs after all. It was bent double by the fall, and it took the strength of the watchman and the two gentlemen to draw it out again. By George! they thought I was spitted beyond hope."

"A foul affair altogether," murmured Carew absently; but the sorry jest was lost in the strident tones of the Chevalier, who now anxiously plied Basil as to the surgeon's opinion of the wound, and expressed himself relieved beyond measure by the reply.

At this juncture Sir John Beddoes, who had drunk enough to inflame his gambler's ardour to boisterous pitch, began to clamour for his promised revenge, and the whole party once more adjourned to the card-room.

In his heart, Basil Jennico would have been genuinely glad to be unsuccessful at the hazard that night; partly from a good-natured dislike to be the cause of the foolish young man's complete ruin, partly from a more personal feeling of superstition. But the luck ran as persistently in his favour as ever.

Carew, with drawn tablets, began loudly to back the winner, challenging all his acquaintance to wager against him. But although the high play and Sir John's increasing excitement and restlessness, as well as the extraordinary good fortune which cleaved to Jennico, soon attracted a circle of watchers, men were chary of courting what seemed certain loss, and Carew found his easy gains not likely further to accrue.

Suddenly the Chevalier, who, with his cheek resting upon his hand, had seemed plunged in deep reflection ever since they had left the supper-room, rose, and with an air of geniality which sat awkwardly enough upon him, cried out to the surprise of all — for he had not been wont to back any player in the club:

"And there is really no one to side with my good friend Beddoes to-night? Why then, Mr. Carew, I will be the man. Thunder-weather, Beddoes," clapping him on the shoulder — "I believe the luck will turn yet; so brave a heart must needs force fortune! What shall it be, Mr. Carew? Something substantial to encourage our friend."

Jennico looked down at the pile of vouchers which lay at his elbow. It amounted already to a terrible sum. Then he looked across at the boy's face, drawn, almost haggard in spite of its youth and chubbiness, and sighed impatiently. He could not advise the fool to go home to bed;

yet for himself he was heartily sick of these winnings. The dice were thrown again, Sir John's hand trembling like a leaf; and again Basil won, and again vouchers were added to the heap.

M. de Ville-Rouge threw a dark glance at the winner as he stepped up to Carew to settle his own debt.

"You should not have backed me," said Sir John ruefully, lifting his eyes from the contemplation of the paper that meant for him another step towards ruin. "The devil's in it; I will play no more to-night!"

"Nay, then," cried the Chevalier, "by your leave I will take your place. I for one am no such believer in the continuance of Mr. Jennico's good luck."

There was something harsh, almost offensive, in the tone of the last words, and Basil turned in surprise towards the speaker.

"The Chevalier," he said, "is very ready to risk his gold against me to-night."

"'Tis so, sir," returned the Chevalier, with such singular arrogance that the watchers looked at each other significantly, and Carew whispered to a young man behind his chair, "Faith, our foreign friend is a bad loser after all!"

Basil had flushed, but he made no reply, and contented himself with raising his eyebrows somewhat contemptuously, while he languidly pushed his own dice-box across the table towards his new opponent.

"Come," said the Chevalier, seizing it and shaking it fiercely, "I will not mince the stake. A hundred guineas on the main."

He threw, and the result of all his rattling being after all the lowest cast of the evening, there was an ill-suppressed titter round the table. Basil made no attempt to hide his smile as he lazily turned over his dice and threw just one higher.

The German's face had grown suffused with dark angry crimson; the veins of his throat and his temples began to swell.

"Double or quits," he cried huskily. He threw and lost; doubled his stake, threw and lost again.

There was something about the scene that aroused the audience to more potent interest than the ordinary nightly repeated spectacle of loss and gain.

The extraordinary passion displayed by the foreigner, not only in his inflamed countenance, but in the very motion of his hands, in the rigid tension of his whole body, presented a strange contrast to the languor of his opponent. It was, moreover, a revelation in one who had been known hitherto as courteous and composed to formality.

"It is to be hoped some one has a lancet," said Carew, "for I believe the gentleman will have an apoplexy unless a little blood be let soon."

"I fear me," answered his companion, "that there will be more blood let than you think for. Did you mark that look?"

At the same instant the Chevalier flung down his box with such violence that the dice, rebounding, flew about the room, and gazed across at Basil with open hatred, as one glad to give vent at last to long-pent-up fury.

"By Heaven, Mr. Jennico!" he cried, "were it not that I have been told how well you have qualified for this success, I should think there was more in such marvellous throwing of dice than met the eye. But your love affairs, I hear, — and I should have borne it in mind, — have been so disastrous, so more than usually disastrous," here his voice broke into a sort of snarl, "as to afford sufficient explanation for the marvel."

There was a cold silence. Then Jennico rose, white as death.

"If you know so much about me, sir," he said

in tones that for all the anger that vibrated in them fell harmoniously upon the ear after the Chevalier's savage outburst, "you should know too that there is a subject upon which I never allow any one to touch. Your first insinuation I pass over with the contempt it deserves, but as regards your observation on what you are pleased to call my love affairs, I can only consider it as an intentional insult. And this is my answer."

The German in his turn had sprung to his feet, but Basil Jennico leant across the table, and before he could guard himself struck him lightly but deliberately across the mouth.

PART III

CHAPTER I

Memoir of Captain Basil Jennico (resumed in the spring of the year 1773)

In my Castle of Tollendhal, March, 1773.

It is the will of one whose wishes are law to me that I should proceed with these pages, begun under such stress of mental trouble, until I bring the tangled story of Basil Jennico's marriage to its singular settlement.

Without, as I now write, all over the land, the ice-bound brooks are melting, and our fields and roads are deep in impassable mud. The whole air is full of the breath of spring, as grateful to the nostrils as it is stirring to the blood of man, to the sap of trees.

But it is ill getting about, for all that the spring-time is so sweet — as sweet and as capricious as a woman wooed — and thus there is time for this occupation of scribe; yet it is a curious task for one bred to so vastly different a trade; neither, God knows, do I find time heavy on my hands just now! Nevertheless, I must even end this preface as I have begun it, and say that I am fain to do as I am bidden.

The last line I traced upon these sheets (I am filled with a good deal of wonder at, and no little admiration of myself, when I view what a goodly mass I have already blackened) was penned at one of the darkest moments of that dark year.

M. de Schreckendorf — little messenger of such ill omen — had but just departed, and in the month that followed his visit the courage had failed me to resume my melancholy record, though truly I had things to relate that a man might consider like to form a more than usually thrilling chapter of autobiography.

Towards the beginning of September, I, still a dweller upon my mother's little property — most peaceful haunt, it would seem, in the heart of our peaceful land — began to find myself the object of a series of murderous attacks — these, so repeated and inveterate, that it was evident that they were dictated by the most deliberate purpose, and the more alarming, perhaps, that I could give then no guess from what quarter they proceeded.

Suspicion fell on a poaching gang, on a dishonest groom, on a discharged bailiff. At length, seeing my mother like to fall ill of the anxiety, I consented to return to London, although the country life and the wholesome excitement of sport had afforded me a relief from my restlessness which existence in the town was far from providing.

No sooner, however, was I fully installed in my London chambers, than the persecution began afresh. I had fallen into an idle habit of going night after night to White's, there to bet and gamble with my modish acquaintances. 'Twas not that the dice had any special attraction for me, but that my nights were so long.

On my way thither one mid-October foggy evening, my life was once more attempted, and this time with a deliberation and ferocity which might well have proved successful at last.

As it was, however, I again providentially escaped, and was able to proceed to the club, where I had an appointment with a poor youth — our Norfolk neighbour, Sir John Beddoes — who had already lost a great deal of money to me, and would not be content until he had lost a great deal more: I had the most insupportable good luck.

I little knew that I should find awaiting me there the greatest danger I had yet to run;

that the head which had directed all these blows in the dark was, de guerre lasse, preparing to attack me in the open, and push its malice to a certain climax. A foreign gentleman — one Chevalier de Ville-Rouge, as I knew him then — had sedulously sought first my acquaintance, and thereupon my company, for some weeks past. And though I had not found him very entertaining — I was not in the mood to be entertained by any one — I had no reason to deny him either the one or the other.

But this night, after first addressing me with looks and tones which began to strike me as unwarrantable, he sat a round of hazard with me, for the sole and determined purpose, as I even then saw, of grossly insulting me. As a reply, I struck him across the face, for, however transparent was the trap laid for me, the provocation before witnesses was of a kind I could not pass over. And, 'fore Heaven, I believe I was in my heart glad of the diversion!

The meeting was fixed for the next morning. Neither of us would consent to delay, and indeed the German's whole demeanour, once he had given a loose rein to his fury, was more that of a wild beast thirsting for blood than of a being endowed with reason.

Both Sir John Beddoes and Mr. Carew, who had formed our party, indignant at the coarseness of the foreigner's behaviour, volunteered on the spot to be my seconds, and Carew, who has a subtle knowledge of the etiquette of honour, arranged the details of our meeting. It was to take place in Chelsea Gardens half an hour after sunrise. The weapons chosen by M. de Ville-Rouge were swords, for although the quarrel had been of his own seeking, my blow had given him the right of choice.

It was two o'clock before I found myself again alone in my rooms that night, my friends having conducted me home, and seeming somewhat loath to retire. I was longing for a couple of hours' solitude before the dawn of the day which might be my last. I felt that my career had reached its turning-point, that this was an event otherwise serious than any of the quarrels in which I had been hitherto embroiled, and that the conduct of affairs was not in my hands.

Carew was anxious about me — he had never yet seen a duellist of my kidney, I believe — and my very quietness puzzled him.

"Make that nutcracker attendant of yours prepare you a hot drink, man," cried he, as at last, with honest Beddoes, he withdrew, "and get to bed. Nothing will steady your hand like a spell of sleep."

But there was no sleep for me. Besides that the pain of the slight wound which I had received in the night's guet-apens was stiffening to great soreness, there was an excitement in my brain — partially due to the fever incident on the hurt — which would not permit the thought of rest.

I had but little business to transact. In view of the present uncertainty of my life, I had recently drawn up a will in which, after certain fitting legacies, I left my great fortune to my wife. Now I merely gathered together the whole of this accumulated narrative of mine into a weighty packet, and after addressing it, deposited it in János's hands with the strict injunction, in the event of my demise, to deliver it personally to Ottilie.

No farewell message would be so eloquent as these pages in which I had laid bare the innermost thoughts of my soul since I first knew her. She should receive no other message from me. I next tore up poor Beddoes's litter of I O U's, and making a parcel of the fragments directed it to him. János received my instructions with his usual taciturn docility, yet if anything could have roused me from the curious state of apathy in which I found myself, it would have been the sight of the dumb concern on the faithful fellow's countenance.

Having thus put all my worldly affairs in order,

I sat me down in my armchair, awaiting the dawn, and viewed the past as one who has done with life. I had a strong presentiment upon me that I should not survive the meeting.

At times, the vision of my wife sleeping, at that very moment, as I had so often watched her sleep, lightly and easily as a child, little wotting, little caring, perhaps, if she had wotted, of her husband's solemn vigil, would rise up before me with a vividness so cruel as well-nigh to rouse me. But the new calmness of my soul defied these assaults; an unknown philosophy had succeeded to the violence of my emotions.

When my seconds called for me in the first greyness of the morning they found me ready for them. They themselves were shivering from the raw cold, with arms thrust to the elbows into the depths of their muffs; Carew, all yellow and shrivelled,— an old man of a sudden,—and Beddoes, blue and purple, the sleep still in his swollen eyes, hardly able to keep his teeth from chattering — a very schoolboy! They could scarce conceal their amazement at my placidity. It was not, indeed, that I found myself bodily fit for the contest, for the whole of my left side was stiff, and I could hardly move that arm without pain; yet placid I was, I scarcely now know why.

Thus we set forth in Sir John Beddoes's coach, János on the box, and a civil, shy young man on the back seat beside Beddoes: this was, the latter informed me, the best surgeon he had been able to secure at such short notice.

The fog disappeared, and when the mists evaporated it promised to be a fine, bright, frosty morning.

Now, it may be after all that I was a little light-headed with the heat of the wound in my blood, for I have no very clear recollections of that morning. It remains in my mind rather as a bright-coloured fantasy than a series of events I have actually lived through.

I remember, as a man may remember a scene in a play, a garden running down to the river-side, very bare and desolate, and the figure and face of my bulky antagonist as he conferred excitedly with two outlandish-looking men, his seconds. These had fierce moustaches, and reminded me vaguely of the cravat captains I had known in the Empire. Then the scene shifts: we stand facing each other. I am glad of the chill of the air, with nothing between it and my fevered breast but the thinness of my shirt. But my opponent stamps like a menacing bull, as if furious at the benumbing blasts. Now I am fighting—fighting for my life — as never in battle or in single combat have I had need to fight before. This is no courteous duel between gentlemen, no honourable meeting, but the struggle of a man with his murderer. Physically at a disadvantage from my hurt, I am moreover conscious that against this brute fury all my skill at arms is of no avail and my strength is rapidly failing. Then, as he drives me by the sheer weight of his mass, I see his face thrust forward into mine, distorted with such a frenzy that I wonder in a sort of unformed way why this man should thus thirst to kill me. The next moment, with an extraordinary sense of universal failure and disorganisation which is yet not pain, I realise that I am hit — badly hit.

Upon that instant I find my brain cleared to a lucidity I have never felt before. I see my opponent's sword flash ruby red with my own blood in the sun rays; I see him smile, a smile of glorious triumph, which cuts a deep dimple beside his lip; I hear him pant at me the strange words, "Ha! Ottilie!" and then I am again seared, rent once more, and to the sound of a howl of many voices my world falls into chaos and exists no more.

* * * * * *

It is sometimes but a short and easy way up to the gates of death, but a long and weary journey back to life. It was a long and weary journey to me.

I was like to a man who travels in the dead of night over rough ways, and now and again slumbers uneasily with troubled dreams, and now looks out upon a glimmer of light in some house or village, and now on nothing but the pitchy darkness; and yet he is always travelling on and on till he is weary with madness of fatigue. And then, as the dawn breaks upon the wanderer, and he sees a strange land around him, so the dawn of what seemed a new existence began to break for me, and I looked upon life anew with wondering eyes.

At first I looked as the traveller may, with eyes so tired and drowsy as scarce to care to notice. But in yet a little while I warmed and quickened to the sun of returning health. I began to be something more than a mere tortured mass of humanity; each breath was no longer misery to draw; the mind was able to re-assert authority over the flesh. That dark, watchful figure that seemed to have been sitting at the foot of my bed for centuries, that was János! Poor old fellow! I could not yet speak to him, but I could smile. My next thought was amaze that I should be in a strange room; it had a very teasing tapestry; its figures had worried me long before I could notice them. In a little while I began to understand that I was not in my own chambers, and to feel such irritation at the liberty which had been taken with me that I should have demanded instant explanation had my strength been equal to the task.

But I come of too vigorous stock, the blood that runs in my veins is too sweet — because I have not, like so many young fools of my day, poisoned it with endless potations and dissoluteness — for me, when once on the broad high road to recovery (to continue my travelling simile), to dally over the ground.

Moreover I was too well nursed. János, it seems, after the first couple of visits, in each of which I was wisely bled of the diminished store the Chevalier's sword had left in my veins — János had had a great quarrel with the surgeon, vowing he would not see his master's murder completed before his eyes and never a chance of hanging the murderer.

It had ended in the old soldier taking the law into his own hands, dismissing the man of medicine, and treating me after his own lights. He had had a fairly good apprenticeship, having attended my uncle through all his campaigns. As far as I am concerned I am convinced that in this, as well as in another matter which I am about to relate, he saved my life.

The other matter has reference to the very change of quarters which had excited my ire, the true explanation of which, however, I did not receive until I was strong enough to entertain visitors. János would give me little or no satisfaction.

"I thought in myself it would be more wholesome for your honour than your other house," was the utmost I could extract. Indeed, he strenuously discouraged all conversation. But the day when this stern guardian first consented to admit Carew and Beddoes to my presence, — and that was not till I could sit up in bed and converse freely, — all that I had been curious about was made clear to me.

Carew, indeed, had the virtue of being an excellent gossip. I had at one time deemed it his only quality, but I learned better then. Both the gentlemen, each in his own fashion, displayed a certain emotion at seeing me again, in which pleasure at the fact of my being still in the land of the living, and likely to remain so, was qualified by the painful impression produced by my altered appearance.

R

Sir John, the boy, sat himself down on the edge of my bed and squeezed my hand in silence, with something like tears in his eyes. Carew, the roué, was very deliberate in his choice of a chair, took snuff with a vast deal of elegant gesture, and fired off, with it might be an excess of merriment, such jocularities as he had gathered ready against the occasion. Both of them seemed to deem it incumbent upon them to avoid any reference to the duel. I, however, very promptly brought up the subject.

"Now, for God's sake," I said, "let a poor man who has been kept like a child with a cross nurse — take your pap, go to sleep, ask no questions — learn at last a little about himself. In the first place, where am I? In the second, what has become of the red devil who brought me to this pass?"

"In the first place, Jennico," said Carew, "you are at the house of Lady Beddoes, mother to our friend here, a very pleasing little residence situate on Richmond Hill. Secondly, that red devil, as you call him, that most damnable villain, has fled the country, as well he might, for if ever a knave deserved stringing up as high as Haman — but of that anon. There is a good deal to tell you if you think you can bear the excitement.

"Well," he pursued, upon my somewhat pettish asseveration, "I myself think a little pleasant conversation will do you more good than harm. To begin with, you are doubtless not aware that you are a dead man."

"How?" cried I, a little startled, for my nerve was yet none of the strongest.

"Nay, nay, dash you, Carew," interposed Sir John, "don't ye make those jokes. Gruesome, I call 'em: it makes me creep! No, Basil, lad, thou art alive, and wilt live to set that Chevalier, whoever he may be, swinging for it yet." And here in his eager partisanship he broke into a volley of execrations which would have run my poor great-uncle's performances pretty close.

"Why," said I impatiently, "'tis enigma to me still why I am here; why I am dead; why the Chevalier should hang. I think you have all sworn to drive me mad among you."

I was so evidently exasperated that Beddoes, all of a tremble, besought Carew to explain the situation.

"He'll do himself a mischief," he cried pathetically; "do you tell him, Carew, — you know what a fool I am!"

Carew was nothing loath to set about what was indeed the chief pleasure of his life, the retailing of scandal; and it seems that the Jennico duel was a very pretty scandal indeed.

"I will take your last question first," said he, settling himself to his task with gusto. "Why the Chevalier should hang? Who he really is, where he comes from, why he hates you with such deadly hatred, Jennico, are all mysteries which I confess myself unable to fathom — doubtless you can furnish us with the clue by-and-by."

As he spoke his pale eye kindled with a most devouring curiosity. Nevertheless as I showed no desire to interrupt him by any little confidence, he proceeded glibly:

"But why the Chevalier should hang is another matter. Gadzooks, I'd run him down myself were it but for his impudence in getting gentlemen like myself to come and see foul play. Why, Jennico, man, don't you know that after charging you like a bull, and running you once through the body, the scoundrel stabbed you again as you were sinking down and the sword had dropped from your hand. I doubt me he would have spitted you a third time to make quite sure, had not Beddoes and I fallen upon him."

"I'd have run him through," here interposed Sir John excitedly; "I had drawn for it, had I not, Dick? — and I'd have run him through, but that the surgeon called out that you were dead; and dash me, between the turn I got and the way those queer seconds of his hustled him away, I lost the chance! And the three of them ran, they ran like rats, to the river. Gad, I'd have left my mark on them even then, but Carew, be hanged to him, held on by my coat-tails."

"'Tis just as Jack told you," said Carew. "No sooner had they heard you were dead, my friend, than they ran for it, and it is quite true that I restrained Jack here from sticking them in the back as they skedaddled. A pretty affair of honour, indeed!"

I lay back on my pillows awhile, musing. I had had time to reflect on many things these days, and — God knows — there were enigmas enough in my life to give me food for reflection. What I had just heard caused me no surprise, tallying as it did with conclusions I had previously reached.

After a moment Carew cleared his throat, edged his chair a foot nearer, and queried confidentially: "Did it never strike you that the Chevalier must have been part and parcel, if not the moving spirit, of those attacks upon your life which you told us of that night at the club? You did not appear to have a notion of it then. Yet there was not a man of us there who did not see but the quarrel was deliberately got up."

"And d'ye mind," cried Sir John, "how he bet me you would not live a month?"

"Ay," said Carew, "and Jennico knows best himself if in his gay youth, in foreign parts, he has not given good cause for this mortal enmity, though to be sure the mystery thickens when we remember how friendly you were with each other. Jennico is such a close dog; he keeps such a dashed tight counsel!"

I smiled. Jennico would keep his counsel still. I meant these good fellows should expound my riddles for me, not I theirs.

"But since I am dead," said I, "I fear, Jack, thou hast lost on me again."

"The gentleman did not leave his address," said Sir John with a grin; and he furtively squeezed my hand to express his secret sense of the little transaction of the I O U's.

"We made some clamour at the Embassy, I promise you," interposed Carew; "we were anxious to pay him all his due, you may be sure. But devil a bit of satisfaction could we get, save indeed that the Ambassador took to his bed with a fit of gout, and you being dead, Jennico,—you are dead still, remember,—to bury you was the best thing your friends could do for you, till you were able to take fit measures to protect yourself. And indeed it was that queer old Tartar of yours, your János, or whatever you call him, who loudly insisted upon your demise, when we found the first alarm was unfounded and that you still breathed. Gad, I believe you have as many lives as a cat! This fellow then says to us in his queer jargon: 'My master lives, but he must all the same be thought dead.' And faith he besought us with such urgency, that, what with seeing you lying there, and knowing what we knew of the foul play that had been practised upon you, we were ready enough to fall in with his desires. Sir John bethought him of his mother's house at Richmond, and offered to accompany you there,—or rather your body: you were little less just then. Next the surgeon swore the journey would kill you, and your servant swore you should not be harboured in the town. The fellow knew you: 'Good breed,' he said, 'not easily killed!' And so he won the day, and Miles the surgeon gave in; but indeed he told me apart, 'twas waste of time disputing, for anyhow you could not see the noon. But here you are at my Lady Beddoes's house at Richmond, alive and like to live, though you have ceased to exist for most men. There was a charming, really a most touching, obituary notice in the Gazettes; you have been duly lamented at the clubs — and forgotten within the usual nine days. Rumours will soon begin to get about of course, but nobody knows anything positive. The secret is still kept. János, I believe, has contrived to assuage the anxiety of your relatives."

Here the speaker took so copious a pinch to refresh himself after his long speech that he set me off sneezing, whereupon my special Cerberus promptly made his appearance and bundled the visitors forth without more ado.

 * * * * * *

I have said that my friend's belief in the Chevalier's implication in the divers murderous onsets that had been made upon me, previous to his own, did not surprise me. The memory of M. de Ville-Rouge's cry, as he dealt me what he believed my death stroke, — a cry in which it would be hard to say whether savage triumph or sheer vindictiveness most predominated, — had come back on me, as soon as I could think at all, with most revealing force.

His arrival in England had coincided with the beginning of the persecution. The look on his face as I had last seen it, that smile and that dimple, had haunted me during long hours of delirium with a most maddening, grotesque, and horrible likeness to the face of her I had so loved. Coupling these things in later sanity of mind with the other evidence, I could not doubt but that here had been some relative of Ottilie, who had interest to put an end to her husband's existence. Had not her pock-marked Mercury at the close of our interview uttered words of earnest warning? ay, I minded them now:

"The matter will not end here. . . . Have a care, young man. . . ."

As I thought of all this, as the whole meaning of what had seemed so mysterious now lay clear before me, I would be seized with a sort of deadly anguish, compared to which all my previous sufferings, whether of body or mind, had been but trivial. Could she, could Ottilie, have *known* of this work? Could she — have *inspired* it?

The sweat that would break out upon me at such a thought was more than all my fever had wrung from my body, and my faithful leech would wonder to find me faint and reeking, and would puzzle his poor brains in vain upon the cause, and decoct me new teas of dreadful compounds, febrifuges which he vowed had never failed.

But then at other times the vision of my wife would rise before me and shame me. I would see again her noble brow, her clear eye, her arched and innocent lip, and in my weakness and the passion of my longing I would turn and weep upon my pillow to think that, having to my sorrow lost her, I should come now to lose even my faith in her, and yet should love her still with such mad love.

Now there must be, as János would have it, something remarkably tough in the breed of Jennico for me to recover from such wounds both bodily and mental. Recover I did, however, in spite of all odds; and a resolve I made with returning strength did a good deal to ease my mind, tossed between such torturing fluctuations.

This resolve was no less than to leave the country some fine morning, in secret, so soon as I could undertake the journey with any likelihood of being able to persevere in it, to speed to Budissin, and discover for myself the real attitude of Ottilie towards me. I was determined that, according as I found her, — either what my heart would still deem her, or yet so base a thing as the fiend whispered, — that I would try to win her back, were I to die in the attempt, or thrust her from my life for ever.

Thus when I heard that my enemy and the world believed me dead, when I realised that she too must probably share in the delusion, I was glad, for not only would it materially facilitate my re-entering the Duchy, but it would afford me an excellent opportunity of judging her real feelings. I had no doubt but that, if I set to work in a proper manner and duly preserved my incognito, I should be able, now that all pretext for quarantine had disappeared, to secure an interview without too much difficulty.

So all my desires hastening towards that goal, I set myself to become a whole man again with so much energy that even János was surprised at the rapidity of my progress.

CHAPTER II

It was towards the middle of December that we started upon the journey — a little sooner indeed than my surgeon and mentor approved of, but his power over me dwindled as my own strength returned.

Being chiefly anxious to preserve my incognito, I hesitated some time before permitting János to accompany me, his personal appearance unfortunately being of a kind unlikely to be forgotten when once seen. But, besides the fact that I could not find it in me to inflict such pain upon that excellent fellow, there was an undoubted advantage to myself in the presence of one upon whose fidelity and courage I could so absolutely reckon in an expedition likely to prove of extreme difficulty and perhaps of peril. Moreover, the man would have followed me in spite of me. I insisted, however, upon his shaving off his great pandour moustaches — a process which though it altered did not improve his appearance; his aspect, indeed, being now so fantastically ugly as to drive me, despite my preoccupation, into inextinguishable paroxysms of laughter every time I unexpectedly got a glimpse of his visage, until habit wore away the impression.

As to myself, my long illness had, as I thought, sufficiently changed me. Besides, the news of my resurrection was too recently and too vaguely rumoured in London to have reached, or to be likely to reach, the Continent for many a long day.

Under the humble style, therefore, of a Munich gentleman returning from his travels, — one Theodor Desberger, with his attendant (now dubbed Johann), a character which my Austrian-German fitly enabled me to sustain, — I set sail from London to Hamburg, and after a favourable sea-passage, which did much to invigorate me, we landed in the free city and proceeded towards Budissin by easy stages; for, despite the ardour of my impatience, I felt the importance of husbanding my newly-acquired strength. At Budissin we put up of course at a different hostelry from that chosen upon our first venture — one much farther away from the palace.

The little town presented now a very different aspect. Indeed, its gay and cheery bustle, and the crisp frosty weather which greeted us there, might have raised inspiring thoughts. But it was with a heart very full of anxiety, with the determination rather to face ill fortune bravely than the hope of good, that I passed the night. I got but little sleep, for, having reached my goal, I scarcely knew how to begin. Nor in the morning had I arrived at any definite conclusion.

The risk of presenting myself in person at the palace after my former fashion was too great to be entertained for a moment. I had therefore to content myself with despatching János to make cautious inquiries as to one Fräulein Pahlen and her relatives, not forgetting a bulky gentleman he knew of, recently returned from England.

I myself, in my plainest suit, and with my cloak disposed as a muffler, partly concealing my face, set forth upon my side to gather what crumbs of information I might.

At the very outset I had a most singular meeting. Traversing the little town in the brisk morning air under a dome of palest blue, I naturally directed my steps towards the castle, seated on its terrace and towering above the citizens' brown roofs.

I had taken a somewhat circuitous route to avoid passing in front of the main guard, and found myself presently in a quiet street, one side of which was bound by the castle garden walls, and the other — that upon which I walked — by a row of private houses seemingly of some importance. Now, as I walked, engaged in gazing upwards at the long row of escutcheoned windows which I could just see above the wall, and foolishly wondering through which of them my cruel little wife might be wont to look forth into the outer world, I nearly collided with a woman who was hurrying out of one of the houses.

As I drew back to recover myself, and to apologise, something in the dark figure struck me with poignant reminiscence. The next instant, as she would have passed me, I caught her by the shoulder.

"Anna!" I cried wildly, "God be thanked, Anna!" For upon this very first morning of my quest Heaven had brought me face to face with no less a person than Ottilie's old nurse.

The recognition on her side was almost simultaneous. No sooner had the muffling cloak fallen from my mouth, than the dull and rather surly countenance that she had turned upon me became convulsed by the most extraordinary emotion. She gave a stifled cry. Then she clapped her hands together, pressed them clasped against her cheek, and stared at me with piercing intensity, crying again and again:

"God in heaven — you! God in heaven — you!"

The black eyes were as hard to read as those

of a shepherd's dog, who fixes with the same earnest look the master he loves or the enemy he suspects. And as we stood thus, the space of a few seconds, my mind misgave me as to whether I had not already jeopardised all my prospects by this impulsive disclosure. It was evident that the woman had heard the story of my death, which in this hostile place was my chief security. But the die was cast, and the chance of information was too precious not to be seized even at greater risks. I laid hold of her cloak, then passionately grasped her hands. "Oh, Anna!" I cried again, and the bare thought that I was once more so near the beloved of my heart brought in my weakness the heat of tears to my eyes. "Where is she? Where is my wife? What does she? Anna, I must see her. My life is in danger in this place; they have tried to kill me because I love her, but I had rather risk death again a thousand times than give her up. Take me to her, Anna!"

The woman had never ceased regarding me with the same enigmatic earnestness; all at once her eyes lightened, she looked from side to side with the cautiousness of some animal conscious of danger, then wrenched her hands out of mine:

"Follow me, sir," she said in a whisper, so urgent in its apprehension as to strike a colder chill into my veins than the wildest scream could have done. Without another glance at me she started off in front, and I as hastily followed, almost mechanically flinging my cloak once more across my mouth as I moved on.

Whither was she leading me? Into the hands of my enemies, whoever they were? — she had always, I had thought, hated me — or into the arms of my wife?

She turned away from the palace, down a bye-street, and then took another turn which brought us into a poor alley where the houses became almost cottages, and where the gutters ran among the cobbles with liquid filth.

My wild hope gave place to sinister foreboding; and as I plodded carefully after her unwavering figure, I loosened the hilt of my sword in its scabbard, and settled the folds of my cloak around my left arm so that at a pinch I might doff it and use it for defence.

Suddenly my guide halted for a second, looked at me over her shoulder, and disappeared down some steps into the open door of a mean little shop. I entered after her, at once disappointed in all my expectations and reassured by the humble vulgarity of the place. Anna, as I had ever known her, was chary of speech. Even, as stooping I made my way into the low, gloomy, and evil-smelling narrow room, I saw her imperiously motion an ugly sallow young woman out of her presence; and, still in silence, I watched her, wondering, as she made fast the doors and bent her dark face to listen if all were still. Then she produced from a counter, paper, ink, and pen, and spreading them out turned to me with a single word: "Write."

So small was the result of all these preliminaries.

"You mean," said I, "that if I write to your mistress, you will convey the letter? Alas! I have written before and she would not even receive my writing. Oh! can you not get me speech of her? I conjure you by the love you bear her, let me see her but for a few minutes."

The woman fixed me for a second with a startled wondering eye, opened her mouth as if to speak, but immediately clapped her hand to it as if to restrain the words. Then, with a passion of entreaty that it was impossible to withstand, she pointed to the paper and cried once more, "Write."

And so I seemed ever destined to communicate with my wife from strange places and by strange messengers.

With a trembling hand and a brain in a whirl I wrote — I hardly know what: a wild, passionate, reproachful appeal, setting forth in incoherent words all I had done and suffered, all my desire, all my faithful love. When I looked up at length I found the black eyes still watching me with the same inscrutable fierceness. I was going to trust my life and its hopes to this woman, and for a moment I hesitated. But at the same instant there was some noise without, and snatching the letter unfinished from before me, she thrust it into her bosom, folded her cloak across it, and stooping close to me demanded in her breathless undertone:

"Where do you live?"

Mechanically I told her, adding: "Ask for M. Desberger."

She nodded with swift comprehension, unbolted the barred front door of the little shop, and drew me hastily out by the back, along a close, flagged passage, leaving an irate customer hammering and clamouring for admittance.

We proceeded through a small yard into another alley, and here she halted a second, still detaining me by my cloak.

"Go home," she said then; "keep close. There is danger — danger. You will hear."

She suddenly caught my hand, kissed it, and was gone. I stood awhile bewildered, astonished, staring, hardly able to grasp the meaning of what had passed, for this last scene in the drama of my life had been acted hurriedly and was full of mysterious significance. Then, unobtrusively, I sought the shelter of my own inn, resolving to obey to the letter the injunctions laid upon me; but fate had willed it otherwise.

Determined not to interfere with the course of fortune by any least indocility, I retired into the seclusion of my chambers, and pretexting a slight indisposition, to rouse no undue suspicion by an air of mystery, gave orders for my dinner to be served there.

A stout red-cheeked wench with rough bare arms had just, grinning, clattered the first greasy dish before me, when I heard János's foot upon the stairs. I had learnt to know the sound of his step pretty well in my recent weeks of sickness, but I had not been wont to hear it come so laggingly, and the fact that it halted altogether outside the door for a second or two, as if its owner hesitated to enter, filled me with such a furious impatience that I got up and flung it open to wrest his news from him. Not even when he had held up my poor great-uncle in his arms to let him draw his last breath on earth, had I seen the fellow wear a countenance of such discomposure.

"In Heaven's name, János," cried I, and the sturdy house-wench turned and stared at him more agoggle and agrin than before.

"Get out of that, you —— " cried my servitor, snapping at her with such sourness, and so forgetful of the decorum he usually displayed in my presence, that it was clear he was mightily moved.

She fled as if some savage old watch-dog had nipped at her heel, and we were alone.

I had returned from my own exploration full of hope, and at the same time of wonder, so that I was at once ill and well prepared for any tidings, however extraordinary. But János's tidings seemed difficult of telling.

"Let us go home, honoured sir," he stammered again and again, surveying me with a compassion and an anxiety he had not vouchsafed upon me at the worst of my illness. I had to drag the words from him piecemeal, as the torturer forces out the unwilling confession.

Yes, he had news — bad news. This was no place for me. It was not wholesome for us here. Let us return to Tollendhal, or Vienna, or even England. Let us start before further mischief overtook us.

I believe I fell upon him at last and shook him. What had he heard. What had he heard of her? I vowed he was driving me mad, vowed that if he did not instantly tell me all I would throw caution to the wind and go to the palace and demand my wife in person, were it of the Duke himself. This threat extorted at length the terrible thing that even the rough old soldier feared to utter.

"The lady," he stammered, "the lady can no longer be spoken of as your honour's wife. She is married."

"Married!" I cried. "What do you mean, you scoundrel? No longer my wife! Married! You are raving — this is stark lunacy."

He shook his grey head under the shower of my fury.

"Married. Does your honour forget that they think here that they have at last succeeded in killing you?"

I looked at him aghast, unwilling to admit the awful illumination that flashed upon my mind. He, believing me still incredulous, proceeded:

"Married she is. Fräulein Pahlen, the lady-in-waiting, — Fräulein Pahlen, as your honour bade me call her, and as it seems she called herself until . . ." and then with a significant emphasis, "until six weeks ago."

"And who is the man?" said I. The words sounded in my ears as if some one else had spoken, but I believe I was astoundingly calm.

Misled no doubt by this appearance of composure, János seemed to take more confidence, and continued in easier tones, while I held myself still to listen.

"It is the Court physician, one privy counsellor Lothner. I was shown his house, a big one in the Schloss Graben, number ten, opposite the palace walls. Ay, yes, they were married six weeks ago, and the Duke was present at the marriage . . . and the Princess too! They say it was made up by their wishes. Oh! honoured sir, let us hence. You are well quit of it all; this is a bad place!"

Yet I stood without moving. Chasm after chasm, horror after horror, seemed to be opening before my mind; chasms so black that I scarce ventured to look into their depths; horrors so unspeakable that I could put no word-shape to them. After Ottilie's messenger had failed to induce me to give up my rights, had come the attempts upon my life, then the duel. The mysterious stranger who had sought to slay me with such rancorous hate, and had called "*Ottilie*" into my dying ears, had returned to claim his bride, and they had wedded in their blood-guilt. Well might the nurse cry and repeat the cry of "God in heaven! God in heaven!"

What new ambush would they now contrive?

"Your honour —————" said János, and he put his hand respectfully upon my sleeve. I caught sight of his frightened face and burst into a fit of rasping laughter.

"Look at your master, János, and see the greatest fool in Christendom! The fool of the play, that is tricked and mocked and beaten from one act to another. Tricked into marrying a serving-maid instead of a princess; tricked into loving her when he should have repudiated her with scorn; abandoned by her when he could no longer live without her; mocked when he sought his wife; driven away by lackeys; stabbed by a murdering hound, a skulking thief in the night! . . . But the last act is only about to begin — every one has had his laugh at the fool, but we shall see, János, we shall see! He laughs best who laughs last, they say. Ten, Schloss Graben, did you say?"

I caught my cloak. I think the faithful fellow actually laid hands upon me to arrest me, but I broke from him as if his clasp had been a straw.

"I'll drive my sword," I remember saying, "into

the first man who dares come between me and my purpose."

And indeed as I fled along the street, scarce knowing what way I took, yet going as straight as a die to my goal, I had no other thought but how clean I would run my blade through the clumsy lumbering brute who deemed he had so well widowed my wife. I had the strength of ten men in me.

CHAPTER III

When I reached the Schloss Graben I stood a moment to reconnoitre, and found myself in the same still, cobble-paved road where I had met Anna a few hours before. On my left rose the high garden-walls overtopped by a web of bare interlacing branches, and over that again the palace windows and its mansard roof; on my right the row of silent brown or red stone houses, well-to-do and snugly private, with beaten iron bars to the low windows and great scallop shells over the doors. This was the house down the stone steps of which my wife's servant had come this morning, and this was number ten. Of course! How clear it was all becoming to me! I dashed the sweat from my brow, for I had come like a lamplighter. Then I tramped up the three steps and again halted a second. How quiet the house was!

But I should soon put some bustle into it, I said to myself, and smiled. I plied the knocker till the sleeping echoes awoke, and I hung on the iron rope of the bell till the shrill protest of the jingling peal rang out into the street. There came other sounds from within as of a flutter in a dovecot. Doors were opened and shut precipitately. A window was thrown back above my head; there was a vision of a white-capped face thrust forward and withdrawn; and, indeed, like rabbits from a warren, most, I believe, of the idle servants in the street were popping out to see whence could proceed such unholy clangour.

The door before me was at length cautiously and slowly opened, and through the aperture the frightened, rose-red face of a maid looked out at me.

I saw that I had been incautious, and therefore addressed her with a suave mock courtesy. Indeed, now that the actual moment had come I felt stealing over me a very deadly calm.

"Forgive me," said I, "my wench, for disturbing you thus rudely. I see I have alarmed you. These are, however, but old soldiers' ways, which I trust your good mistress will pardon to an old friend. Your mistress is, if I mistake not, now the doctor's lady. But when I knew her she was Fräulein Ottilie Pahlen."

The girl's mouth had, during this long speech, which in my new mood came glibly enough to my lips, become broadened into a grin. There are very few girls in the Empire, I have been told, that will not feel mollified towards a soldier.

"Is your mistress within?" I pursued.

She dropped a curtsey, and after a comprehensive glance over my person threw open the door. Would the gentleman walk in? She brought me through a brick-paved hall into a long low oak-panelled room, all dark and yet all shining with polish. It was very hot from a high china stove.

"What visitor shall I announce to the gracious lady?" she asked, sidling towards me, and thrusting her apple face as forward as she dared.

"I am so old a friend, in fact, I may say so near a connection, that I should like to give your gracious lady a pleasant surprise," said I; "I will not therefore give my name." As a propitiatory after-thought, I pinched the hard red cheek and dropped a coin into her apron pocket. I tried to make my smile very sweet, but it felt stiff upon my lips. She, however, saw nought amiss, and pattered out well content.

Then followed a few minutes' waiting; all had grown still again around me. Through the deep recessed windows I looked forth into a little court-yard with one bare tree. This, then, was the home Ottilie had chosen instead of an English estate, instead of Tollendhal, instead of all I could offer her in courtly Vienna or great London! How she must love this man! Or was it only the plebeian instinct reasserting itself in spite of all? . . . The Court doctor's lady!

I heard a footfall on the bare-boarded stair, and with a smile that was this time the natural expression of the complicated bitterness of my soul, I moved a few steps so as to place myself in the best light.

My wife was, perhaps, still in ignorance of my escape from death. Anna had not yet carried her grievous news of the failure of their endeavours. Indeed, this was evident from the general placidity of the household, as well as the staid regularity of the approaching steps. To witness her joy at the discovery was sufficient revenge for the moment. After that the reckoning would be with — well, with my successor.

Such was the state of my thoughts at the crucial moment of my strange story.

I have said that I was calm, but during the little pause that took place between the cessation of the footsteps and the turning of the lock I could hear the beating of my own heart like the measured roar of a drum in battle.

Then was the door opened, and before me stood — not Ottilie, who had been my Ottilie, but the other Ottilie, the Princess! She was advancing upon me with the old well-remembered gracious smile, when all at once she halted with much the same terror-stricken look with which Anna earlier in the day had recognised me, and clasped her hands, crying:

"God be merciful to us, M. de Jennico!" and seemed the next instant ready to burst into tears.

In the first confusion of my thoughts, in the rage created by this eternal *quid pro quo*,—that I should ever find the lady-in-waiting when I wanted the Princess, and the Princess when I wanted the lady-in-waiting,—I might have been inclined to think that Anna had after all spread her tidings, and that my wife's former mistress had come to her aid at this awkward moment; but the surprise and consternation on this woman's countenance were too genuine to have been counterfeit.

Whatever reason brought the Princess here I was in no humour to inquire.

"I came to see my wife, Madam," said I, "and not to presume upon your Highness's condescension. I am determined to see my wife," I insisted; "that Ottilie Pahlen, who was your maid of honour, and lived with me as my wife for a month, as your Highness well knows, and who was in such haste to wed this Court doctor of yours at the first rumour of her husband's death."

I spoke in a very uncourtier-like rage. But she

whom I addressed showed neither anger nor astonishment, but sank into the nearest chair, a mere heap of soft distressed womanhood, wringing her plump dimpled hands, while tears of extraordinary size suffused her eyes and overflowed upon her cheeks.

At sight of this my heat fell away; I threw myself on my knees beside her, and, all forgetful of the distance between us, took one of her hands in mine and poured forth an appeal.

"You were always kind to me; be kind now. I must see my wife. I have been cruelly treated; I am surrounded with enemies; be you my friend!"

She leant forward and looked at me earnestly with swimming eyes.

"Is it possible," she exclaimed — "is it possible, M. de Jennico, that you have not found out yet? . . . that you do not suspect? . . ."

Even as she spoke, and while I knelt looking up at her, the scales fell from my eyes. I needed no further word. I knew. How was it possible, indeed, that I should not have known before? I saw as in a flash that this comely burgher woman was not, had never been, never could have been, the Princess. I saw that the hand I still unconsciously held bore marks of household toil, that on the third finger glittered a new wedding ring. Then a thousand memories rushed into my mind, a thousand confirmatory details. Oh, blind — blind — blind that I had been — fool, and worse than fool! The mystery of my wife's mocking smile; the secret that had so often hung unspoken on her lips; her careless pretty ways; the depth of her injured pride; and then the manner in which she had been guarded from me, the force employed against me, the secret diplomatic attempts to free her, followed, on their failure, by the relentless determination to do away with me altogether! Before my reeling brain it all rose into towering conviction — a joy, a sorrow, both too keen for humanity to bear, seized upon my weakened frame. I heard as if in the far distance the words the woman near me was saying:

"It all began by a freak of her Highness, . . ." and with the echo of them whirling as it were in a mad dance through my brain to the sound of thundering cataracts, a whirlpool of flame spreading before my eyes, I fell with a crash, as it seemed, into a yawning black abyss.

When I again came to myself the cold air was blowing in upon me through the open casement, and I was stretched full length on a hard floor, in what seemed a perfect deluge of the very strongest vinegar I have ever smelt. At one side of me knelt my hostess, her healthy face blanched almost beyond recognition. On the other, between my wandering gaze and the window, swam the visage of the maid, eyes and mouth as round as horror could make them, but with cheeks the ruddiness of which, it seemed, no emotion could mitigate.

Both my kind attendants gave a cry as I opened my eyes.

"He is recovering, Trude," said Madam Lothner (to call her now by her proper name).

"Ah! gracious lady," answered the wench in an unctuous tone of importance; "his face is still as red as the beet I was pickling when I heard you scream — would God the master were here to bleed him. Shall I send into the town to seek him?"

"God forbid!" cried her mistress, in a hasty and peremptory tone. "No, I tell you, Trude, he is recovering, and I have not been a doctor's wife these six weeks for nothing. The flush is fading even as I look at him. See thee here, fetch me some of the cordial water."

I do not know how far her six weeks' association with the medical luminary, her husband, had profited Madam Lothner. I have since been told that her administration of cordial, immediately

T

upon such a blood stroke to the head as mine, ought really to have finished me off. But as it happened it did me a vast deal of good, and I was soon able to shake off the giddiness, the sickness, and the general confusion of my system.

With recovered wits it gradually became apparent to me that while Madam Lothner continued to ply me with every assistance she could think of, regarding me with eyes in which shone most kindly and womanly benevolence, her chief anxiety nevertheless was to get rid of me with all possible despatch.

But I was not likely to give up such an opportunity. The chaos in my mind consequent upon the unexpected revelation, and its disastrous physical effect, was such as to render me no very coherent inquisitor. Nevertheless, the determination to learn all that this woman could tell me about my wife rose predominant above the seething of my thoughts.

Ottilie, my wife, was Ottilie the Princess after all! I had felt the truth before it had been told me. But whilst they removed an agonising supposition, these struck me nevertheless as strange unhomely tidings which opened fresh difficulties in my path — difficulties the full import of which were every second more strongly borne upon me.

Ottilie the Princess! ... Everything was changed, and the relentless attitude of the Princess bore a very different aspect to the mere resentment of the injured wife. When my letters had been flung back in my face, when I had been kidnapped and expelled the country, it had been then by her orders. She had sent to demand the divorce. Who had set the bravo on my track? By whose wish had my life been so basely, so persistently, attempted? By hers — Ottilie, the Princess? A Princess who had repented of her freak, whose pride, whose reputation, had suffered from the stigma of an unequal match.

The man whose sword had twice passed through my body had called out, "Ha! Ottilie!" Who dare call on a Princess thus save her kinsman or — her lover?

I felt the blood surge through me again, but this time in my anger it brought a sense of courage and strength. I interrupted Madam Lothner as, with a joyful exclamation that I was now quite restored, she was about to issue an order for the summary fetching of a hired coach.

"Let your maid go," said I authoritatively, "but not for a coach. I have yet much to say to you."

I was without pity for the distress this demand occasioned, deaf to the hurried whisper:

"For pity's sake, go now that you can. You are in danger here. Think of yourself, if you will not think of me!"

"I can think of but one person," said I harshly. "I have come a thousand miles to learn things which I know you can tell me, and here I remain until I have heard them. Any delay on your side will only prolong the danger, since danger there be."

She looked up in tearful pleading, met my obstinate gaze, and instantly submitted — a woman born to be ruled.

"Go, Trude," she said faintly, "and warn me if you see your master coming. What will she think of me?" sighed the poor lady as the door closed upon an awe-struck but evidently suspicious Trude. "But no matter, better that just now than the truth. Now, sir, for God's sake, what is it you would have of me?"

"Let me go back," said I, "to the beginning. When I married . . . my wife at Tollendhal, she was then, for a freak as you say, acting the lady-in-waiting, while you assumed her rôle of Princess?"

"It is so," said Madam Lothner, "but I never

knew till the deed was accomplished to what length her Highness had chosen to push her folly. I could not then attempt to interfere or advise, still less could I be the person to send tidings to the Court."

"So?" said I, as she paused.

"So," said she, "in great fear and trembling, I deemed it best to obey her Highness's strict command, and await events at the Castle of Schreckendorf, still in my assumed part."

"But when my wife returned to you," I said, and my voice shook, "returned to you in a peasant's cart, — oh, I know all about it, Madam, I know that I drove her forth through the most insensate pride that ever lost soul its paradise, — when she returned, the truth must have already been known?"

"Ach, yes," murmured the sentimental Saxon, her eyes watering with very sympathy at the sight of my bitter self-reproach. "Yes, it was because of rumours which had already reached the residence (from your friends in England, I believe), that his Serene Highness the Duke sent in such haste to recall us. He would not come himself for fear of giving weight to the scandal. But it was her Highness who chose to confirm the report."

"How?" cried I eagerly.

"Why, sir," answered the doctor's lady, flowing on not unwillingly in her soft guttural, though visibly perturbed nevertheless, and now and again anxiously alive to any sound without — "why, sir, her Highness having returned to Schreckendorf before the arrival of the ladies and gentlemen from Lausitz, and being, it seemed, determined" — here she hesitated and glanced at me timidly — "determined not to return to Tollendhal ever again, her Highness might easily, had she wished, have denied the whole story. And indeed," continued the speaker with a shrewdness I would not have given her credit for, "had she so behaved it would have best pleased her relations. But she was not so made."

"Ah, no indeed," said I, "her pride would not stoop to that."

"You are right," said Madam Lothner, with a sigh, "she is very proud. She was calm and seemed to have quite made up her mind. 'I will give no explanation to any one,' she said to me, 'and I recognise in no one the right to question me. But my father shall know that I am married, and that I am separated from my husband for ever. I am not the first woman of my rank on whom such a fate has fallen.' That was her attitude."

And here the good creature broke forth as if in spite of herself with passionate expostulation.

"Ah, M. de Jennico, but she suffered! Oh, if you would atone, leave her now, leave her at least in peace! You have brought enough sorrow already into her life. Ach! I do not know how it has been between you; but now that she thinks you dead, for God's sake let it be!"

"By Heaven, Madam," cried I, half mad, I believe, between pain, remorse, and fury, "these are strange counsels! Do you forget that we are man and wife, and this by her own doing? But truly I need not be surprised, for you do not hesitate before crime at the Court of Lausitz, and if murder be so lightly condoned, sure it is that bigamy must seem a very peccadillo."

Madam Lothner stared at me with startled eyes and dropping jaw.

"Murder," she whispered, "M. de Jennico! what terrible thing do you say?"

Then she put her hand to her head, ejaculating: "True, it was the Margrave himself who brought us news of your death on his return from England. It was in the English papers. I feared I know not what, but this — this — God save us!"

I looked at her in fresh bewilderment. She was as one seized by overwhelming terror. I felt that her emotion had its origin in causes still unknown to me.

"And who is the Margrave?" I cried quickly.

She lowered her voice to the barest breath of sound, and glanced fearfully over her shoulder as if afraid of eavesdroppers even in this retired room.

"Prince Eugen, as they call him," she said, "one of her Highness's cousins. He has, I do not quite know how, hopes of sovereignty in Poland, and they were to have been married: it was her father's wish, and it is so still."

I sprang up with an imprecation, but the lady almost flung herself upon me, and clapped her hand over my mouth.

"In the name of God," she said, "be still, or you will ruin us! My husband is his most devoted adherent. In this house he rules, and we bow to the earth before him."

I sank back into my seat, docile, in spite of myself, impressed by the strength of her fear. New trains of revelations crowded upon me. Eugen of Liegnitz-Rothenburg — Rothenburg — Ville-Rouge — I saw it all!

She went on, bringing her mouth close to my ear:

"The Princess hated him, and indeed he has

grown into a strange and terrifying man, so oddly impulsive, cruel, wilful, vindictive. He always professed to love the Princess, but I cannot but think that it was the love of taming — he would dearly love to break her, just as he loves to break the proudest-spirited horse. His grey eye makes me grow cold. As I said, from a child she hated him, and it was for that — having seen one whom she thought she could love . . ." Here she paused, and glanced at me, and hesitated.

It was for that. I remembered. She had told me of the unhappy fate that threatened "the Princess" that evening when we met under the fir-trees to decide upon my crazy match, and when, as I had deemed, she had fooled me to the top of my bent. She had spoken in tones of scathing contempt and hatred of some cavalier. And now? Suddenly gripped by the old devil of doubt and jealousy, I cried out, "And now, after all, the fate of being wedded to an obscure gentleman seems to her more dreadful than that of sharing her place with her cousin, and the peculiar qualities of the hated relative have been very usefully employed in ridding her of the inconvenient husband? Oh, Madam, of course you know your Court of Lausitz, and I think I begin to see your drift: you think, in your amiability, that it would be preferable to see your mistress bigamously united, than that she should legitimise her position by yet another and more successful attempt at assassination."

"I fail to understand you, sir," drawing back from me, nevertheless, with a glance of mistrust and indignation.

"I will be plain," said I: "when the Princess, who is my wife, left me, — I will own I bear some blame, but then I had been strangely played with, — she had doubtless already begun to repent what you call her freak. When I followed her and implored her forgiveness, — you yourself know all about it, Madam, for you must have acted under her orders, — she flung back my letters, through your agency, with a contemptuous denial of any knowledge of such a person as M. de Jennico. When I wrote to her, her whom I believed to bear your name, a pleading, abject letter, for I was still but a poor loving fool, her only answer was to have me seized and driven from the country like a criminal. Later on, when I refused to be a party to her petition for divorce, she thought, no doubt, she had given me chances enough, and this time she deputed the noble bully, her cousin, to manage the matter in his own fashion. My life was attempted five times,

Madam. And when it all failed,— your Prince Eugen, you tell me, he was in England, and there was a certain great bulky Chevalier de Ville-Rouge, who particularly sought my acquaintance — 'tis he, is it not? — your Prince Eugen honoured me by seeking a duello, and by running his august sword through my common body, and that more often, be it said, than custom sanctions in honourable encounters. I was given for dead. No wonder! It seems to be the sport of hell to keep me alive. I can scarce think it is the will of Heaven."

Madam Lothner had followed my tirade with what appeared the most conflicting sentiments: blank astonishment, horror, indignation. It was the last, however, that predominated. Her countenance became suffused with crimson; her blue eyes flashed a fire I had not deemed them capable of harbouring; she forgot the precautions she herself had so strenuously enjoined.

"And do you dare, sir," cried she, "accuse my mistress of these things — you, whom she loved? You knew her as your wife for four weeks, and yet you know her so little as to believe her plotting your death! Those letters, sir, you speak of, she never received, nor did I, nor did she nor I ever hear of your presence in this land. 'Tis true that after you had left, — for *you* left her first, remember, — after well-nigh a year without tidings of you, she did herself send to you to request the annulment of the marriage. It was *to free you* because she believed you repented of it, and she felt she had entrapped you into it. And when, sir, you refused, she had hope again in her heart, for she loved you. And she suffered persecution on your account, and was kept and watched like a state prisoner — she that had always lived for the free air, and for her own way. They were cruel to her, and put dreadful pressure upon her that she should make her appeal alone to the Pope. But she held firm, and bore it all in silence, and lived surrounded by spies, her old friends and old servants banished from her sight, until the news came that you were dead. Then . . . ah, then, she mourned as never a woman mourned yet for her first and only love! As to marriage — what dreadful things have you been saying? Her Highness will never marry again. She will be faithful as long as she lives to you, whom she believes dead. And God forbid it should be otherwise, for Prince Eugen would wed her from no love, I believe, but solely to punish her for resisting him so long, to break her to his will at last, and triumph over her. Oh, no, she would never wed again! You must believe me, for I have been with her through it all, and though she would mock me and laugh at me once, she turned to me afterwards as to her only friend —— Get up, M. de Jennico, get up! Ach Gott! what a coil this is! My good sir, get up; think if the doctor were to come in! Ach Gott! what is that you say? Nay, I have been a fool, and this is the worst of all. My poor friend, there is no room for happiness here!"

For I had fallen at her feet again, and was covering her hand with kisses, blessing her with tears, I believe, for the happiness of this moment.

She ended, good soul, by weeping with me, or rather, over the pity of the joy that was doomed, as she thought, to such brief duration.

"Oh, you are mad, you are mad!" she said, as I poured forth I know not what extravagant plans. Ottilie loved me, cried I in the depths of my exultant soul: what could be difficult now? "You are mad! Have you not yet learned your lesson? Do you not understand that they will never, *never* let you have her? Go back to your home, sir, and if you love her never let her know you are still alive, for if they heard it here, God knows what she would be put to bear; and if she knew they had tried to murder you, it would kill her.

I tell you, sir, a Court is a dreadful place, and Prince Eugen, you know what he is, and his Serene Highness himself, he is hard as the stones of the street. You have seen what they have done — no law can reach them! They will not fail again. And if a second scandal —— " she paused, hesitated, shuddered, then bending over to me she whispered, half inarticulately, "if a second scandal came to pass, who knows what forfeit she might not have to pay!"

But I rose, clasped her two hands, and looked into her eyes with all the bold joy that filled my heart.

"My kind friend," I said, "you cannot frighten me now. Keep you but our secret, and you will yet see your mistress happy." I wrung her hands, and hurried to the door, as eager now to be gone as I had been to enter. I must act, and act at once, and there was much to do.

She followed me, lamenting and entreating, to the steps, where stood faithful Trude, with garments blown about in the cold wind. But, as I turned to take a last farewell, my hostess caught me by the sleeve.

"Keep close," she said, "keep close; and if you are hurt, if you are ill —— " she hesitated a second, then leaned forward and breathed into my ear, "do not send for the Court doctor."

CHAPTER IV

I RUSHED out into the street, treading as if on air, my cloak floating behind me, my head thrown back, all warnings unheeded in the first overpowering tide of this joy which had come upon me at the darkest hour of all.

I had told myself that I must act, and act at once. But till I had had a moment's breathing time to realise the extraordinary revelations by which the whole face of the past and of the future was changed to me, I could form no coherent thought, much less could I form plans.

I wanted space for this — space and solitude. And so I hurried along as I have described, looking neither to the right nor to the left, when I was seized upon from behind, and by no means gentle hands brought me first to a standstill, and next threw the folds of my cloak around me in such a fashion as once more to cover my face.

"Are you mad?" said János, with a fiercer display of anger than I had ever known him show to me, though he had marshalled me pretty rigidly through my illness. "I have been following you these five minutes, and all the town stares at your honour. 'Tis lucky you took a side turning just now or you would have been straight into the great place, perhaps into the main guard. If you want to look for death, you can go to the wars like my old master, but 'tis an ill thing to find it in the assassin's blade, as I thought you had learned by now. Do you forget," continued János, scolding more vehemently, "that they are all leagued against you in this country? Do you forget how they packed you out of the land last year, and warned you never to return? 'Tis very well to risk one's life, but 'tis ill to throw it away."

"Oh, János, true soul," said I, as soon as I could get air to speak with, for his grasp upon the folds of my cloak was like an iron clamp, "all is changed, all is explained. You saw me last the most miserable of men: you see me now the happiest!"

We had paused in a deserted alley leading into the gardens on the ramparts. As I looked round I saw that the sky had grown darkly overcast, and by János's pinched face, as well as by the bowing and bending of the trees, that the wind had risen strong and cold. To me it might have been the softest breeze of spring. I drew the man over to a bench all frosted already by tiny flakes which fell persistently, yet sparsely, and there I told him my tale of joy. He listened, blinking and grinning. At length when it was duly borne in upon him that the wife I was seeking was really and actually the Princess of the land, he clasped his hands and cried with a certain savage enthusiasm:

"Oh, that my old master had lived to see the day!" But the next instant the bristling difficulties of the situation began to oppress his aged heart. He pondered with a falling face.

"Then your honour is in even greater danger than I had thought," said he, "and every second he passes in this town of cut-throats adds to the risk."

"Even so," said I, clapping him on the shoulders, my spirits rising higher, it seemed, with every fresh attempt to depress them, — "Even so, my good fellow; and therefore since my wife I mean to have, and since I mean to live to be happy with her, what say you to our carrying her off this very night?"

He made no outcry: he knew the breed (he himself had said it) too well. As you may see a dog watch his master's signal to dash after the prey, wagging his tail faintly the while, so the fellow turned and fixed me.

"And how will your honour do it?" said he without a protest.

"How?" said I, and laughed aloud; "by my soul I know not! I know nothing yet, but we will home to the inn and deliberate. There is nought so difficult but love will find the way, and Romeos will scale walls to reach their Juliets so long as this old world lasts."

I rose as I spoke, and so did János, shaking the snow from his bent shoulders.

"I know nothing of the gentlemen your honour speaks of, nor of the ladies, but my old master, your honour's uncle, did things in his days. . . . God forgive me that I should remember them against a holy soul in heaven! There was a time when he kept a whole siege (it was before Reichenberg in '59) — a whole siege waiting, ordered a cessation of fire for a night, that he might visit some lady in the town. He was the general of the besieging army, and he could order as he pleased. By Saint Stephen, he got into the town somehow . . . and I with him . . . and next morning we got out again! No one knew where we had been but himself, and myself, and herself — he, he! — and before midday we had that town."

"Fie, fie, János," said I, "these are sad tales of a field-marshal; let us hope my good aunt never heard them."

"Her Excellency," said János, and crossed himself, "would have gloried in the deed. But, your honour, we have the heavens against us to-night; I have not seen a sky look blacker, even in England, since the great storm at Tollendhal. . . . Ah, your honour remembers when."

"All the better," said I, as we turned the corner; "a stormy night is the best of nights for a bold deed."

And I thought within myself: "I lost her in the storm; in the storm shall I find her again." Thus does a glad heart frame his own omen.

It was all very fine to talk of carrying off my wife in such fashion; but when, seated together near the fire in my room, talking in whispers so that not even the great stove door could catch the meaning of our conclave, János and I discussed our plans, we found that everything fell before the insuperable difficulty of our ignorance of the topography of the palace. There seemed nothing for it but to endeavour to interview Anna once more, dangerous as the process might be. And we were already discussing in what character János should present himself, when Fortune — that jade that had long turned so cold a shoulder upon me — came to the rescue in the person of the good woman herself. There was a hard knock at the door, which made us both, conspirators as we were, jump apart, and I involuntarily felt for the pistol in my coat skirts, whilst János stalked to open.

And there stood the lank black figure which had once seemed to cast a sort of shadow on my young delight, but which now I greeted as that of an angel of deliverance. She loved her mistress, her mistress loved me — what could she do me then but good?

I sprang forward and drew her in by both hands. She threw back the folds of her hood and looked round upon us, and her grim anxious countenance relaxed into something like a smile. Then she dropped me a stiff curtsey, and coming close to my ear:

"I gave my mistress the gracious master's letter," she said, and paused. I seized upon her hand again.

"Oh, Anna, dear Anna, how is she? How did she take it? Was she much concerned? Was she . . ." I hesitated, "was she glad to learn I am not dead?"

The woman's eyes looked as if they would fain speak volumes, but her taciturn tongue gave utterance to few words.

"My mistress," she said, "wept much, and thanked God." That was all, but I was satisfied.

"She is in much fear for you," the messenger went on after a pause. "She bade me say she dared not write because of the danger to you; she bade me say that the danger is greater than you know of; that your enemies are other than you think. Now they believe you dead, but you may be recognised. And you were out to-day again!" said Anna, suddenly dropping the sing-song whisper of her recitation and turning upon me sternly with uplifted finger. "Out, in spite of my warning! I know, for I came to the inn to find you. All this is foolish."

"And this is the end of your message?" said I, who had been drinking in every word my wife's sweet lips had so sweetly spoken for me. "Was there nothing else?" said I again, for my soul hungered for a further sign of love.

"There was one thing more," said Anna in her stolid way: "she bade me say she would contrive to see you somehow soon, but that as you love her you must keep hidden."

I shut my eyes for a second to taste in the secret of my heart the honeyed savour of that little phrase that meant so much: *"as you love me!"* for there rang the unmistakable appeal of love to love! And I smiled to think that she still reserved the telling of her secret. I guessed it was because she was pleased that I should want her for herself, and not for the vain pride that had been our undoing.

And then, with my bold resolve a thousandfold strengthened, I caught Anna by the arm.

"Now listen," said I, and stooped to bring my lips to her ear. "When I went out this afternoon it was to good purpose. I have seen Frau Lothner. . . . I know all."

"Lord God!" cried Anna, and snatched her hand from mine and threw her arms to heaven, her long brown face overspread with pallor; "and she has seen you, has recognised you — the Court doctor's wife! Then God help us all! If the secret is not out to-day it will be to-morrow. Oh, my poor child, my poor child!" She rocked herself to and fro in a paroxysm of indignant grief.

"But," said I, trying to soothe her that she might listen to my plan, "Madam Lothner is an old friend of mine, she is devoted to the Princess, she has a kind heart, she has promised me discretion."

"She!" said Anna, and paused to throw me a look of unutterable scorn. "She, the sheephead! in the hands of such an one as the Court doctor! My lord, I give you but to midnight to escape! for as it happens — and God is merciful that it happens so — the Margrave has sent for the doctor at his camp of Liegnitz, and he will not return until after supper."

"So be it," said I gaily; "escape I shall, Anna, but not alone."

The woman's sallow face grew paler yet. The depth of the love for the child she had nursed at her breast gave her perspicacity. Her eye sought mine with fearful anticipation.

I drew her to the furthest end of the room and rapidly expounded my project, which developed itself in my mind even as I spoke. Outside the snow was falling fast. All good citizens were within doors; there was as yet no suspicion of my presence in the town; the palace was quiet and my bitterest enemy was absent; to delay would be to lose our only chance. The passion of my arguments, none the less forcible, perhaps, because of the stress of circumstances which kept my voice at whisper pitch, bore down Anna's protests, her peasant's fears. I had, I believe, a powerful auxiliary in the woman's knowledge of all that her beloved mistress might be made to suffer upon the discovery of my reappearance. She felt the convincing truth of my statement, that if the attempt was to be made at all it must be made this very night, and she saw too that I said true when I told her I would only give up such attempt with my life.

Moreover (joy as yet hardly realised!) she knew that my wife's happiness lay in me alone; and so she agreed, with unexpected heartiness, to every detail of my scheme.

She was to meet me at the end of the palace garden lane before the stroke of eight, two hours hence, and admit me through a side postern into the garden itself. We were obliged to fix so early an hour to avoid the necessity of running twice past sentries, who, it seemed, were doubled around the palace after eight o'clock. The Princess's apartments were upon the first floor on the garden side, and from the terrace below it was quite possible, it appeared, for an active man to climb up to her balcony. I would bring a rope-ladder — János should make it, for he had no doubt some knowledge of that scaling implement. As soon as she had shown me the way, Anna was to endeavour to prepare her mistress for my coming. János in his turn was to be waiting with my carriage and post-horses as near the garden gate as he dared. The Princess, the nurse told me, was wont to retire about nine, it might be a little earlier or later, and liked then to be left in solitude, Anna herself being the only person admitted to her chamber.

Among the many risks there was one inevitable, the danger of being discovered by my wife lurking on her balcony before Anna had had time to carry her message: for it was impossible, the woman warned me, that she should now see her mistress before the latter descended to meet the Duke at supper. I was, however, gaily prepared to face this risk, and even, foolhardy as it may seem, desired in my inmost soul that there should be no intermediary on this occasion, and that my lips only should woo her back to me; that this first meeting after our hard parting should be sacred to ourselves alone.

I reckoned besides upon the fact that since Ottilie knew I was in the town, she would not be surprised at my boldness, however desperate; that she would ascertain with her own eyes who it was who dared climb so high, before she called for help.

At length, when everything was clear,—and the woman showed after all a wonderful mother wit,— Anna departed in the storm, and I and János were left to our own plans and preparations. As for me, my heart had never ridden so high; never for a second did I pause or hesitate. In a few minutes we had devised half a dozen alternate schemes of flight, all equally good — all equally precarious.

"Will your honour leave it to me," said the old campaigner at last, as he sat beginning to plait and knot various lengths of our luggage ropes into an escape ladder, — "the settlement of the inn account, the post-horses, and the choice of the road?"

With this I was content.

The wind had abated a little, but the snow was still falling steadily when I set forth at length. The streets were, as I expected, very empty, and the few wayfarers whom I chanced to meet were so enveloped and so plastered with white, the chief thought of every one was so obviously how best to keep himself warm, how soonest to get within shelter, that I hugged myself again upon my luck. There was a glow within me which defied the elements.

At the corner of the garden lane, at the appointed place, even as the tower clock began the quarter chimes, I saw a woman's figure rapidly approaching the trysting spot from the opposite direction. I hesitated for a moment, uncertain as to its identity, but it made straight for me, and I saw it was Anna. As we turned into the lane itself she suddenly whispered:

"Put your arm round my waist," and the next

instant, from the very midst of my amazement, I realised her meaning: we had to pass close by a sentry-box. Woman's wits are ever sharper than man's. The sentry was stamping to and fro, beating his breast with his disengaged hand, but ceased his bear dance to stare at us, as we came within the light of the postern lamp, and launched at the dim couple so lovingly embraced some rude witticism in his peasant tongue, accompanied by a grunt of good-natured laughter. My supposed sweetheart pulled her hood further over her face, answered back tartly with a couple of words in the country dialect; and, followed by an ironical blessing from the churl, we were free to pursue our way unchallenged.

This was the only obstacle we encountered; the lane was quite deserted. We stopped before a little postern door half buried in ivy, which Anna, producing a key from her pocket, unlocked after some difficulty. At last it rolled back on its rusty hinges with what sounded in my ears as an exultant creak. An ancient bird's nest fell upon my head as we passed through into the garden. Anna carefully pushed the door to once more, but without locking it, and we hastened towards the distant gleaming front of the palace, stumbling as we went, for the soft snow concealed the irregularities of the path. Without hesitation, however, my guide led me between two fantastically carved hedges of box and yew till we came to a statue, rearing a blurred outline, ghostly white in the faint snowlight. Here she stood still and pointing to the south wing:

"There," she said, while all the blood in my body leaped, "there are my mistress's apartments; see you those three windows above the terrace? The middle window with the balcony is that of her Highness's bedroom. You cannot mistake it. The ivy is as thick as a man's arm, and you may climb by it in safety. Now that I have done what you bade me I will go to the palace. God see us through this mad night's work!"

With these words she left me. I ventured to the foot of the terrace wall, and creeping alongside soon found the terrace steps, which I ascended with a tread as noiseless as the fall of the thick snowflakes all around me. I stood under her balcony. I groped for the ivy-stems, and found them indeed as thick as cables. It was a plant of centenarian growth, and it clasped the old palace walls with a hundred arms, as close as welded iron: as strong and commodious a ladder as my purpose required. I swung myself up (I tremble now to think how recklessly, when one false step might have ended the life that had grown so dear), and next I found myself upon the balcony — Ottilie's balcony! — and through the parted curtains could peer into her lighted room.

Then for the first time I paused, hesitating to pry upon her retirement like a thief in the night. For a moment I knelt upon the snow and cried in my heart for pardon to her. Then, drawing cautiously aside from the shaft of light, I looked in. It was a large lofty apartment with much gilding, tarnished it seemed by time, and with faded paintings and medallions on the walls. In an alcove curtained off I divined in the shadow a great carved bed, whose gilt curves caught now and again a gleam of ruby light from the open door of an immense rose china stove. My eyes lingered tenderly over every detail of the sanctuary sacred to my lady. Outside upon the balcony, all in the darkness, the cold, and the snow, my whole being began to swim in a dreamy warmth of love. It is like enough that had not something come to rouse me, I might have been found next morning, stiff, frozen upon my perch, with a smile upon my lips — a very sweet and easy death! But from this dangerous dreaminess I was presently aroused to vivid watchfulness and energy.

My wandering gaze had been for a little while uncomprehendingly fixed upon a shining wing of flowered satin stuff that trailed on one side of a great armchair, the back of which was turned towards me. This wing of brocade caught the full illumination of the candles on the wall and showed hues of pink and green as dainty as the monthly roses in the garden of my old home in England. Now as I gazed the roses began to move as if a breeze had shaken them, and lo! the next moment, a little hand as white as milk fluttered down like a dove upon them and drew them out of sight. For a second my heart stood still, and then beat against my breast like a frantic wild thing of the woods against the bars of its cage. She was there, there already, my beloved! What kept me from breaking in upon her, I cannot say — a sort of fear of looking upon her face again in the midst of my great longing — or maybe my good angel! Anyhow I paused, and pausing was saved. For in a second more a door opposite to me opened, and an elderly lady, followed by two servants carrying a table spread for a repast, entered the room. The lady came towards the armchair and curtsied. I saw her lips move and caught the murmur of her voice, and listened next in vain for the music of those tones for which my ear had hungered so many days and nights.

I saw the white hand cleave the air again as if with an impatient gesture. The lady curtsied, the lackeys deposited the table near the chair, and all three withdrew.

I had trusted to fate to be kind to me this night, but I had not dared expect from fate more than neutrality; and now it was clear that it was taking sides for me, and that my wife had been strangely well inspired to sup in her chamber alone, instead of in public with her father, as I had been told was her wont.

No sooner had the attendants retired than I beheld her light figure spring up with the old bounding impetuosity I had loved and laughed at, fling herself against the door, and I heard the snap of the key. Now was my opportunity! And yet again I hesitated and watched. My face was pressed against the glass in the full glare of the light, without a thought of caution, forgetting that, were she to look up and see me, the woman alone might well scream at the wild, eager face watching her with burning eyes from out of the black night. But she did not look up.

Wheeling round at the door itself as if she could not even wait to get back to her chair, Ottilie —

my Ottilie — drew from beneath the lace folds that crossed upon her young bosom a folded letter, which I recognized, by the coarse grey paper, as that which my own hand had scored in the little provision shop a few hours ago.

An extraordinary mixture of emotions seized upon my soul: a sort of shame of myself again for spying upon her private life, and an unutterable rapture. I could have knelt once more in the snow as before a sacred shrine, and I could have broken down a fortress to get to her. From the very strength of the conflict I was motionless, with all my life still in my eyes.

When she had finished reading she lifted her face for a moment, and then for the first time I saw it. Oh, dear face, paled with many tears and dark thoughts, but beautiful, beyond even my heated fancy, with a new beauty, rarer and more exquisite than it is given me to describe! The same, yet not the same! The wife I had left had been a wilful and wayward child, a mocking sprite — the wife I here found again was a gracious, a ripe and tender woman, upon whose lips and eyes sat the seal of a noble, sorrowful endurance.

She lifted the letter to her lips and kissed it, looked up again, and then our eyes met! Then I hardly remember what I did. I was unconscious of any deliberate thought; I only knew that there was my wife, and that not another second should pass before I had her in my arms.

I suppose I must have hurled myself against the casement; the lock yielded, and the window flew open. Enveloped in a whirl of floating snow I leaped into the warm room. With dilated, fixed eyes, with parted lips, she stood, terror-stricken, at first, yet erect and undaunted. I had counted all along on her courage, and it did not fail me! But before I had even time to speak, such a change came over her as is like the first upspring of sunlight upon the colourless world of dawn. As you may see a wave gather itself aloft to break upon the shore, so she drew herself up and flung herself, melting into tears, body and soul, as it were, upon my heart. And the next moment her lips sought mine.

Never before had she so come to me — never before had life held for me such a moment! Oh, my God! it was worth the suffering!

x

CHAPTER V

A knock without aroused us. With a stifled cry of alarm, the woman who had made no sound on the violent entry of an armed man upon her unprotected solitude, now fell into deadly anguish. She sprang to the door, and I could see the lace on her bosom flutter with the fear of her heart as she bent her ear to listen. The knock was repeated.

"Who is it?" cried Ottilie, in a strangled voice. "I had said I would be alone."

"'Tis I, child," came the answer in the well-known deep note; "it is Anna, alone."

I thrust my sword back into its scabbard; my wife drew a long breath of relief, and glanced at me with her hand pressed to her heart.

"Anna, thank God! We can admit her: Anna is safe," she said, and turned the key.

Anna opened the door, stood an instant on the threshold, contemplating us in silence; a faint smile hovered about her hard mouth. Then, without wasting words on futile warnings, she made fast the lock, deposited on the floor a dark lantern she had concealed under her apron, walked to the window, which she closed as best she could, and drew the curtains securely. Indeed, her precaution was not idle: through the silence of the outside world of night, muffled by the snow, but yet unmistakable, the tread of the first patrolling round now grew even more distinctly upon our ear, passed under the terrace, emphasised by an occasional click of steel, and died away round the corner. With the vanishing sound melted the new anxiety which had clutched me, and I blessed the falling snow which must have hidden again, as soon as registered, the tell-tale traces of my footsteps below.

Anna had listened with frowning brow; when all was still once more, she turned to the Princess, and briefly, but in that softened voice I remembered of old:

"I have told your ladies that you had bidden me attend to you this night, and that you must not be disturbed in the morning," and then turned to me: "All is ready, sir; we have till noon before being discovered. And now, child," she continued, as Ottilie, still closely clinging to my side, looked up inquiringly, "no time to lose; there is death in this for thy gracious lord, if not for us all as well."

"What does she mean?" asked Ottilie, and

seemed brought from a far sphere of bliss face to face with cold reality. "Oh, Basil, Basil, to leave me again!"

"Leave you! I will never leave you," cried I, touched to the quick at the change which had come upon the proud spirit of my beloved; "but if you will not come with me, with your husband, if you fear the perils of flight, the hardships of the road, or even," said I, though it was only to try her and taste once again the exquisite joy of loving, humble words from her lips, "if you cannot make up your mind to give up your high state here, to live as the wife of a simple gentleman, I am content to die at your side. But leave you, never again! Ah! my God, once was too much."

She looked at me for a second with tender reproach in her tear-dimmed eyes and upon her trembling lips; then she answered with a simplicity that rebuked my mock humility:

"I am content to go with you, Basil, were it to the end of the world."

At this I could not, in spite of Anna's presence, but take her to my heart again, and the nurse, after watching us with a curious look of mingled pleasure and jealousy in her hollow eyes, suddenly and somewhat harshly bade us remember once more that time was short.

"You," she went on to her lady, peremptorily, as if conscious of being herself the true mistress of the situation, "drink you of that broth and break some bread, and drink of that wine, for you have not eaten to-day. And you," she added, turning to me, "make ready with your ladder."

Impatiently and sternly she stood by us until we prepared to obey her orders.

We owe a very great debt of gratitude to this woman!

My wife sat down like a child, watching me, sweet heart! over every mouthful of soup as one who fears the vision may fade. As for me, appreciating all the importance of immediate action, I threw from me the perilous temptation of letting myself go to the delight of the moment — a delight enhanced, perhaps, by the very knowledge of environing danger. Opening my cloak, I unwound the length of rope from my waist, cautiously slipped out again on the balcony and fastened one end to the iron rail. Remembering the precious burden it was to bear, I could not be satisfied without testing every knot, and finally trying its strength with my own weight by descending to the terrace. It worked satisfactorily, and the distance, fortunately, was not excessive. Then leaving it dangling, in three leaps I was up again and once more in the warm room, just in time to see an exquisite gleam of silk stocking disappear into the depths of the fur boot which Anna was fastening with all the dexterity of a nurse dressing a child.

And, indeed, my sweet love submitted to be turned and bustled and manipulated with an uncomplaining docility as if she was again back in her babyhood — although in truth I have reason to believe, from what I know of her and have heard since, that not even then had she ever been remarkable for docility.

Grimly smiling, Anna completed her labour by submerging the dainty head in a deep hood; the sable-lined cloak and the muff she handed over to me with the abrupt command: "Throw them out! Auswerfen!" Anna should have been a grenadier sergeant; nevertheless, the thought was good, and I promptly obeyed. Next she gave me the lantern — she had thought of everything! — and commenced extinguishing the lights in the room. I took Ottilie by the hand, the little warm hand, ungloved, that it might the tighter feel the rope.

"Will you trust yourself, love?" said I. She gave me no answer but a shaft of one of her old fearless looks and yielded her waist to my arm, and thus we stepped forth into the snow and the night. I guided her to the rope and showed her where to hold, and where to place her feet, and then, climbing over the balcony, supporting myself by the projecting stones and the knotted ivy, I was able to guide the slender body down each swinging rung: for when the blood is hot and the heart on fire one can do things that would otherwise appear well-nigh impossible.

Safely we reached the ground. I enveloped her in the cloak which Anna's forethought had provided, and after granting myself the luxury of another embrace I was preparing to ascend the blessed rope again for the purpose of assisting Anna, when I discovered that incomparable woman solidly and stolidly planted by our side in the snow.

"All is right, gracious sir," she said in a hoarse whisper; "but it would be as well to take away that rope, since you can go up and down so easily without it."

Recognising in an instant the wisdom of the suggestion — it was well some one had a waking brain that night! — I clambered up once more, and in a few seconds had flung down the tell-tale ladder, and descended again.

Anna took up the lantern, which she hid under

her cloak, and, all three clinging together, we hastened to the postern as noiselessly as shadows. The snow fell, but the wind had all subsided, and the air was now so still that the cold struck no chill.

Outside the postern, seeing no one in sight, we paused.

"I have told János to be at the bottom of the lane," said I to Anna, as she pocketed the key after turning the lock. And then to my wife, who hung close and silent to my arm: "It is but a little way, and then you shall rest."

Even as I spoke I turned to lead her, but Anna arrested me:

"I have thought better," she said. "To leave the town in a carriage is dangerous. I have arranged otherwise."

I was about, I believe, to protest, or at least discuss, when Ottilie, who had hitherto permitted herself to be led whither I would, like one in a dream, suddenly cried to me in an urgent undertone to let Anna have her way: "Believe me," she said, "you will not repent it." I would have gone anywhere at the command of that voice.

"It shall be so," said I; "but there is János, and we cannot leave him in the lurch."

"No, we must have János with us," said Anna;

"but that is easy. Follow me, children." And uncovering her lantern, with her skirts well kilted up, she preceded us with fearless strides to the secluded turn at the bottom of the lane, where, true to his promise, I found the heiduck and his conveyance.

For the greater security the lamps of the carriage had not been lit, but we could see its bulk rise in denser black against the gloom before us, and feel the warmth of the horses steam out upon us, with a pleasant stable odour, into the purity of the air.

There was a rapid colloquy between our two old servants. János, the cunning fox! at once and appreciatively agreed to Anna's superior plan of action, and indeed his old campaigner's wits promptly went one better than the peasant's shrewdness: instead of merely dismissing the carriage as she suggested, he bade the coachman drive out by the East Gate of the town and, halting at Gleiwitz, await at the main hostelry there the party that would come on the morrow. And in the dark I could see him emphasise the order by the transfer of some pieces, that clicked knowingly in the night silence. The point of the manœuvre, however, was only manifest to me when, turning to follow Anna's lead again down a side alley, the fellow breathed into my ear with a chuckle:

"While your honour was away I took upon myself to despatch his carriage with our luggage, to meet us, I said, at Dresden. That will be two false scents for them — and we, it seems, take the south road to Prague! We shall puzzle Budissin yet."

On we tramped through the deserted bye-streets. It was only when we were stopped at last, in that self-same poor little mean lane, before the self-same poor little mean shop, faintly lit inside by a dull oil lamp, that I recognised the scene of my morning's interview with Anna — that interview which seemed already to have passed into the far regions of my memory, so much had I lived through since.

We met but few folk upon our way, who paid little attention to us. As we entered into the evil-smelling room, stepping down into it from the street, and as Anna shot back the slide of the lantern and turned upon us a triumphant smiling face, I felt that our chief peril was over. The shop was empty, but she was not disposed to allow us even a little halt: she marshalled us through the dank narrow passages with which I had already made acquaintance, across the courtyard into the back street. There stood a country waggon with a leathern tent. By the flash of the lantern I saw that to it were harnessed a pair of great raw-boned chestnuts that hung their heads patiently beneath the snow, yet seemed to have known better service in their days — no doubt at one time had felt the trooper's spurs.

Beside them stood a squat man, enveloped to the ears in sheepskin, with a limp felt hat drawn over his brow till only some three-quarters of a shrewd, empurpled, not unkindly visage was left visible. The waggoner was evidently expecting us, for he came forward, withdrew his pipe, touched his hat, and made a leg.

"My cousin," said Anna to us, and added briefly and significantly: "He asks no questions."

Then in a severe tone of command she proceeded to address several to him. Had he placed fresh hay in the waggon according to her orders? Had he received from her sister the ham, and the wine and the blankets? Had the horses been well fed? On receiving affirmative grunts in answer, she bade him then immediately produce the chair, that the lady and the gentleman might get in.

Between the closed borders of her hood I caught a glimpse of Ottilie's faint smile, as lighted by the lantern rays she mounted upon the wooden stool and disappeared into the dark recesses of the waggon, stirring up a warm dust as she went, and a far-away fragrance of hay and faded clover.

"Now you, sir," said Anna, and jogged my elbow.

I believe at that moment we were to her but a pair of babes and nurslings for whom she was responsible, and that she would have as readily combed our hair and washed our faces as if we were still of a size to be lifted on her knee.

I obeyed. And truly, as I crawled forward in the dark, amid the warm straw, groping my way to the further end till I laid my hand on Ottilie's soft young arm extended towards me, when I heard her laugh a little laugh to herself as we snuggled in the nest together, I felt a happiness that was like that of a child, all innocent of past and improvident of future. Nevertheless at one and the same time my whole being was stirred to its depths with a tenderness my manhood had not yet known.

In those foolish bygone days I had loved her, the sweet soul, with the unworthy, mad passion of a lover for his mistress. When she left me I had mourned her as a man mourns for his wife, flesh of his flesh, bone of his bone. Now, however, we seemed to be lad and maid together; our love, after all the sorrow and the agony we had passed through, seemed to wear the unspeakable freshness of a first courtship. It was written that good measure was to be paid me to compensate for past anguish — good measure, heaped up, flowing over! I took it with a thankful heart.

The cart swayed and creaked as János and Anna mounted and settled themselves at our feet, drawing the hay high over themselves. Then came another creaking and swaying in the forward end, we heard a jingle of bells, a crack of the whip and a hoarse shout: the cart groaned and strained to the effort of the horses, then yielded. And at a grave pace we rumbled over the cobblestones, turning hither and thither through street after street which we could not see. And in the midst of our hay we felt a sense of comfortable irresponsibility and delicious mystery. All in the inner darkness we were dimly conscious of the snowy pageant outside: the ghost-like houses and the twinkling lights. Ottilie lay against my shoulder, and I felt her light breath upon my cheek.

After a while — it would be hard to say how long — there was a halt; there came a shout from our driver, and an answering shout beyond. I knew we had come to the Town Gates. That was a palpitating moment of anxiety as the two voices exchanged parley, which the heavy beating of the pulses in my ears would not allow me to follow. Next the rough cadence of a jovial laugh fell loud upon the air, and then — sweeter music I have seldom heard! — the clank of the gate's bar. Once more we felt ourselves rumbling on slowly till we had passed the bridge and exchanged the cobbles of the town for the surface of the great Imperial road, more lenient for all its ruts. The cousin cracked his whip again and bellowed to his cattle; after infinite persuasion they broke into a heavy jog-trot.

"In the name of the Father, and of the Son, and of the Holy Ghost," said Anna suddenly from her dark corner, in a loud vibrating voice, "give thanks to God, you children!" She leant forward as she spoke, and pulled aside the leathern curtains that hung across the back of the cart.

With the rush of snowy air came to us framed by the aperture a retreating vision of Budissin, studded here and there with rare gleams of light.

Thus did my wife, the young Princess of Lusatia, leave her father's dominions, her prospects of a throne, for the love of a simple English gentleman!

CHAPTER VI

I SHALL carry to the grave, as one of the sweetest of my life, the memory of that night journey. Coming as it did between the fierce emotions and dangers of our meeting and flight, and the perilous and furious episode that yet awaited us, it seems doubly impregnated with an exquisite serenity of happiness. Full of brief moments, that brought me then a poignant joy, it brings to my heart as I look back on it now a tenderness as of smiles and tears together.

After a little while the flakes had ceased falling, and, in the faint snowlight, beneath a clear sky, we gazed forth together from our ambulant nest, here upon mysterious stretches of plain-land, there upon ghosts of serried trees, trees that marched as it were past us back towards Budissin. I remember how in a clear space of sky a star shone out upon us at last, and how it seemed a good omen, and how we kissed in the darkness.

Then there was our meal, with Anna's lantern to illumine the feast. I was so lost in watching my beloved bite her black bread contentedly with small white teeth, and toast me with loving eyes over the thin wine, that I could scarce fall to, myself. Yet when I did so it was with right good appetite, for I was hungered, and I never tasted better fare.

Then János got out of the waggon to sit in front by the driver and smoke. My great-uncle had been such a confirmed tobacco-man that János had acquired the habit in attendance upon him, and it did not behove me to interfere with an indulgence fostered by thirty years' service.

Anyhow, on that night the stray whiffs of his strong tobacco mingled not unpleasantly with the keen cold scents of the night; and the sound of the two men's talk, with the monotonous jingle and rumble of harness and cart, made a comfortable human accompaniment to our passage in the midst of the great silence. Anna went to sleep and snored after her good day's work, waking now and again with a start and a groan, and thence to oblivion once more. And then we too, oblivious of the world, fell into a long dream, hand in hand — a great wide-eyed dream filling our silence with soaring music, our darkness with all the warm colour of life.

And thus we reached the first halting-place in the itinerary planned by János and myself on the

Imperial Chaussée. The place whence we would best defy our enemies, and therefore our ultimate destination, was of course my own Castle of Tollendhal, recent experience having sufficiently demonstrated that in England we should be ill-protected from the machinations of Budissin. This first stage was Löbau.

Never did town look so thoroughly asleep under its snow-laden eaves, behind its black shutters, thought I, as our tired horses, steaming and stumbling, dragged our cart up the main street.

A watchman had just sung out his cry: "The twelfth hour of the night, and a clear heaven," when we turned into the market-place, from the middle of which he chanted his informing ditty to those Löbauers who might chance to be awake to hear and thereby be comforted.

Spear in one hand and lantern in the other, the fellow approached to inquire into such an unusual event as the passage of midnight travellers. We heard János, in brief tones, tell a plausible tale of his lordship's travelling coach having broken down (on its way from Görlitz, said he, who never missed a chance of falsifying a scent!), and of his lordship, who happened to be in a special haste to proceed, having availed himself of a passing country cart to pursue his journey to the next posting town, and so forth, all the main points of this story being corroborated by an affirmative growl from our Jehu. Whereupon the watchman, honest fellow, nothing loath doubtless to vary the perennial monotony of his avocation, undertook to awaken for our benefit the inmates of the post-house, the best house of entertainment, he asseverated, in the town.

It will be long, I take it, before the worthy burghers of Löbau, and especially mine host of the "Cross Keys," forget the mysterious passage at dead of night of the great unknown magnate and his hooded lady, of the tire-woman with the forbidding countenance, and of the ugly body-servant, whose combined peremptoriness and lavish generosity produced such wonders, — even had subsequent events not sufficed to fix it upon their minds as a tragic epoch in the history of their country.

A few minutes of obstinate hammering and bell-ringing by János and by the deeply impressed watchman, awoke the hostelry from the depths of its slumbers. The bark of dogs responded first to the clangour; lights appeared at various corners; windows, and then doors, were thrown open. At last János threw back the leather curtain of our conveyance, and hat in hand, with his greatest air of bonne maison assisted my lord in his cloak, my lady in the furs (both much ornamented with wisps of hay), to alight from their cart.

My lady, veiled and silent, retired for an hour's rest, and so away from the peering curiosity of the assembling servants. And my lord paced the common-room, feverishly waiting for the coming of the new conveyance which János, after one of his brief requisitioning interviews (pandour style), had announced would be forthcoming with brief delay.

The common-room was dank and cold enough, but my lord's soul was in warm consorting: it was still exalted by the last look that my lady had thrown back at him, raising her hood for one instant as, ascending the stairs, she had left him for the first separation.

In less than an hour the tinkling of collar-bells and the sound of horses' hoofs, clattering with a vigour of the best augury, were heard approaching. Even as János entered to confirm by word the success of his quest, my beloved appeared with a readiness which to me was sweeter than any words: she too had been watching the moments which would speed us onwards together once more.

Through a pretty concourse of dependants, all of whom had now got wind of the rain of gratuities with which the great traveller's servant eased the wheels of difficulty, we entered our new chariot. I can hardly mind now what sort of a vehicle this was. I believe in its days it had been a decent enough travelling chaise: at any rate it moved fast. Once more we rolled through the silent street, on the hillside roads, up hill and down dale, my bride warmly nestled in my arms, and both of us telling over again the tangled tale of the year that had been wasted for us.

And thus, in the idle iteration of lovers' talk, with the framing of plans for the future, changeable and bright as the clouds of a summer's day, did we fill the rapid hours which brought us to Zittau in the early morning.

But Zittau was still within the dominions of the eloping Princess's father; and at Zittau, therefore, much the same procedure was hastily adopted as at the previous stage: another hour or so of separation, another chaise and fresh horses, and once more a flight along the mountain roads, as the dawn was spreading grey and chill over the first spurs of the Lusatian hills.

This time we spoke but little to each other. The fatigue of a great reaction was upon us. Anna was already snoring in her corner, her head completely enveloped in her shawl, when, as I gazed down tenderly at my wife's face, I saw the sweet lids close in the very middle of a smile, and the placidity of sleep fall upon her.

I have had, since the Budissin events, many joys; but there is none the savour of which dwells with so subtle, so delicate, a perfume in my memory as that of my drive in the first dawn with my wife asleep in my arms.

It was not yet twelve hours since I had found her; and during those twelve hours I had only seen her in the turmoil of emotion, or under stress of anxiety, or by some flitting lamplight. Her image dwelt in my mind as I had first beheld it through the glass of the palace window, lovely in the first bloom of graceful womanhood, stately amid the natural surroundings of her rank. Now, wrapped in confident slumber, swathed in her great robes of fur, the only thing visible of her young body being the little head resting in the hollow of my arm, the fair skin flushing faintly in the repose of sleep, fresh even in the searching cruelty of the growing light, like the petal of a tea rose, the rhythmic pulse of her bosom faintly beating against my heart, she was once more, for a little while, to me the Ottilie I had held in my castle at Tollendhal. And as, for fear of disturbing her, I restrained my passionate longing to kiss those parted lips, those closed lids with the soft long eyelashes, I could not tell which I yearned for most: the Princess, the ripe woman I had found again . . . or the wayward mistress playing at wife I had schooled myself to banish in the wasted days of my overweening vanity.

But why thus linger over the first stage of that happy journey? Joy can only be told by contrast to misery. We can explain sorrow in a hundred pages, but if delight cannot be told in one, it cannot be told at all. It is too elusive to be kept within the meshes of many words. Sorrows we forget, — by a merciful dispensation, — and it may be wholesome to keep their remembrance in books. Joys ever cling to the phials of memory like a scent which nought can obliterate.

And since I have undertaken to record the reconquest of Jennico's happiness, there remains yet to tell the manner in which it all but foundered in the haven. For this heartwhole ecstasy of mine could not last in its entirety beyond a few brief moments. As I thus grasped my happiness, with a mind free at last from the confusing vapours of haste and excitement, even as the fair world around us emerged sharp and bright from amid the shadows of dawn, all the precariousness of our situation became likewise defined. Between me and the woman I loved, though now I held her locked in my arms, arose the everlasting menace of separation. How long would we be left together? Where could I fly with her to keep her safe? I hoped that amid the feudal state of my castle I could defy persecution, but what could such a life be at best? Thus, in the very first sweetness of our reunion, was felt the bitterness of that hidden suspense that must eventually poison all.

Now as I look back, nothing seems more dreamlike than the way in which my boding thought suddenly assumed the reality of actual event.

"In a little while" (I was saying to myself, as I watched the shadows shorten, and the beams of sunlight grow broader upon the snow), "in a little while the hounds will be started in pursuit, the old persecution will be resumed, more devilish than ever." And at the thought, against my will, a contraction shook the arm on which my love was resting. She stirred and awoke, at first bewildered, then smiling at me. I let down the glass of the coach, that the brisk morning air might blow in upon us and freshen our tired limbs.

We were then advancing but slowly, being midway up the slope of a great wide dale; the horses toiled and steamed. And then as we tasted keenly the vigorous freshness of the morning air, and looked forth, speechless, upon the beauty of the waking hour of nature — that incomparable hour so few of us wot of — there came into the great silence, broken only by the straining of harness and the faint thud of our horses' hoofs in the snow, another noise: a curious, faint, little, far-off noise like to no sound of nature. Ottilie glanced at me, and I saw the pupil of her eye dilate. She uttered no word, neither did I. But, all at once, we knew that there was some one galloping behind us.

I thrust my head out. János was already on the alert: standing with his back to the horses, leaning upon the top of the coach, he was looking earnestly down the valley. I can see his face still, all wrinkled and puckered together in the effort of peering against the first level rays of the sun. Now, as I leaned out also, and the horse's gallop grew nearer and nearer upon my ear, I caught, as I thought, a faint accompaniment of other hoofs, still more distant. I looked at János, who brought down his eyes to mine.

"But three altogether, my lord," he said. And, reaching as he spoke for his musketoon, he laid it on top of the coach. "And, thank God," he added, "one can see a long way down this slope." He bade the driver draw up on one side of the road, and I was able myself to look straight into the valley.

A flying figure, that grew every second larger and blacker against the white expanse beneath us, was rushing up towards us with almost incredible swiftness. In the absolute stillness of the world locked in snow, the rhythm of the hoofs, the squelching of the saddle, the laboured snorting of the over-driven horse, were already audible. There were not many seconds to spare — and action followed thought as prompt as flash and sound. There was only time, in fact, to place the bewildered Anna, just awakened, by my wife's side at the back of the coach, to pull up the shutter of both windows, and to leap out.

I was hatless. I grasped my still sheathed sword in one hand, and with the other fumbled for my pistols in my coat skirts, whilst with a thrust of my shoulder I clapped the coach door to. There was not time even to exchange a word with Ottilie, but her deathly pallor struck me to the heart and fired me to the most murderous resolve.

And now all happened quicker than words can follow. No sooner had I touched the ground, than out of space as it were, roaring and reeking, hugely black against the sunshine, the horse and his rider were upon me. I had failed to draw my pistol, but I had shaken the scabbard off my sword. There seemed scarce a blade's length between me and the flying onslaught. Suddenly, however, the great animal swerved upon one side, and was pulled up, almost crouching on its haunches, by the force of an iron hand. The rider's face, outlined against the horse's steaming neck, bent towards me: Prince Eugen's — great indeed would have been my surprise had it been any other — ensanguined, distorted with fury, glowing with vindictive triumph, as once before I had seen it thus thrust into mine.

"Thou dog, Jennico . . . ill-slaughtered interloper . . . at last I have got thee! Out of my way thou goest this time! . . ."

As it spat these words, incoherently, the red face became blocked from my view by a fist outstretched, and I found myself looking down the black mouth of a pistol barrel. I cut at it with my sword, even as the yellow flame leaped out: my blade was shattered and flew, burring, overhead. But the ball passed me. At the same instant there came a shout from above; the Prince looked up and, quick as thought, wrenched at his horse; the noble beast rose, beating the air with his forefeet, just as János fired, over my head.

For a second all was confusion. The air seemed full of plunging hoofs and blinding smoke. Our own horses, taking fright, dragged the carriage some yards away, where it stuck in a snowheap. Then things became clear again. I saw, — I know not how, — but all in the same flash, I saw a few paces beyond me, János now standing in the road, my wife in her dishevelled furs behind him; and in front, free from the bulk of his dying horse, my enemy on foot, pistol in hand, and once more covering me with the most determined deliberation of aim. With my bladeless sword hilt hanging bracelet-like on my sprained wrist, defenceless, I stood, dizzily, facing my doom.

Then for a third time the air rang with a shattering explosion. The Prince flung both arms up, and I saw his great body founder headforemost, a mere mass of clay, almost at my feet. I turned again, and there was my János, with the smoking musketoon still to his cheek, and there also my wife with the face of an avenging angel, one hand upon his shoulder, and the other, with unerring gesture of command, still pointing at the space beyond me where but a second before stood the enemy who had held my life on the play of his forefinger.

CHAPTER VII

For the space of a few seconds we three stood motionless. The awful stillness of the shadow of death was upon our souls. Then, approaching from the distance came again to our ears the sound of hoofs, the stumbling trot of a tired horse; and the quick wits of János were awakened to action.

"Into the carriage, my lady," said he, "and you, my lord! We have loosed enough shots for one day, and so it is best we should move on again and avoid these other gentlemen."

He smiled as he spoke, a grim, triumphant smile. As for me, it was certes nothing less than triumph I felt in my heart. I would have had Prince Eugen dead, indeed, but not so, not so!

"Let us, at least," I cried a little wildly, "see if he still breathes!"

"No need, my lord;" and János caught me by the wrist. "I am not so old yet," he added, eyeing his weapon with a delighted look, "but what I can still aim straight. Did I not know him to be as truly carrion now as his good horse itself, poor beast, I would surely enough despatch him as he lies there biting the mud. But no need, my lord. Right in the heart! The man was dead before he touched the ground." And as he spoke János dragged us towards the coach.

The driver, half risen from his seat, still clutching one rein, seemed struck into an imbecility of terror; the horses, now quieted, stretching their necks luxuriously against the loosened bits, were sniffing at the snow, as if in the hope of lighting upon a blade of grass. Anna sat on the steps, her face blanched to a sort of grey.

"Up with you!" said János, and pushed her with his knee. "Do you not see your lady is faint?" The words aroused her, and they roused me. In truth, Ottilie seemed scarcely able to sustain herself; it was time I carried her away from such scenes.

After closing the doors, János handed me the musketoon and the cartouche-box, with the brief remark: "His lordship had better load again, the while I drive, for this coachman of ours is out of his wits with fright." And thus we started once more; and in the crash and rattle of the speed to which János mercilessly put the horses, the stumbling paces of the approaching pursuers were lost to our hearing. The draught of air across her face revived Ottilie, who now sat up with courage, and tried to smile at me, though her face was still set in a curious hardness, whilst I, with the best ability of a sprained wrist, reloaded and reprimed. Events (as I have oft thought since) had proved how happy a thought it had been of mine (some two weeks before, when we made our preparations to leave London, to gratify my good János's desire for one of those admirable double-barrels I had seen him so appreciatively and so covetously handle at Fargus and Manton's, in Soho.

When we reached the neck of the valley, I leaned out again and looked back. The scene of that crisis in my eventful life lay already some hundred yards below us. The second of our pursuers — a dragoon of Liegnitz, as I now could see by his white coat, dirty yellow against the snow — was in the act of dismounting from his exhausted steed. I watched him bend over the prostrate figure of his chief for an instant or two; then straighten himself to gaze up at our retreating coach; then, with his arms behind him and his legs apart, in what, even at that distance, I could see was an attitude of philosophical indifference, turn towards the approaching figure of his comrade, who, some hundred yards further down, now made his appearance on the road, crawling onwards on an obviously foundered horse. It was evident that whatever admiration the Margrave may have commanded during his lifetime, his death did not inspire his followers with any burning desire to avenge it.

I leant out further and handed back the loaded musketoon to János.

"You may spare our horses now," said I; "there is no fear of further pursuit to-day."

"Ay, my lord, so I see," responded the heiduck, with a cheerful jerk of the head in our rear. "And, moreover, in a quarter of an hour we shall be across the border."

* * * * * *

Now of our story there is little more to tell. And well for us that it is so; for one may, as I have said, chronicle strange adventures and perils of life and limb, and one may pour out on paper the sorrows of an aching heart, the frenzy of despair; but the sweet intimate details of happiness must be kept secret and sacred, not only from the pen but from the tongue. It will not, however, come amiss that, to complete my narrative — in which, one day, if Heaven will, my children shall learn the romance of their parents' wooing and marriage — I should set down how it came about that the Margrave contrived (to his own undoing) to track us so speedily; how, with his death, came the dispelling of the shadows upon both our lives.

Shortly after our return to Tollendhal, a letter reached my wife from the other Ottilie. It was evidently written in the greatest distraction of mind, upon the very morning after our escape from Budissin. Although conversation may not have been a strong point with Madam Lothner, she seemed to wield a very fluent pen. She took two large sheets to inform us how, upon her husband's return on the previous night, his suspicions being by some unaccountable means awakened, he had forced from her the confession of all that had passed between us in the afternoon. I cannot here take up my space and time with the record of her excuses, her anguish, her points of exclamation, her appeals to Heaven to witness the innocence of her intentions. But when I read her missive I understood Anna's contemptuous prophecy: "She keep a secret? the sheep-head!" I understood also my wife's attitude of tolerant affection, and I blushed when I remembered the time when, blinded by conceit, I had sought this great mock-pearl, when the real jewel lay at my hand. . . . But to proceed.

The doctor had instantly given the alarm at the palace, with the result that the Princess's flight was discovered within two hours after it had taken place. Now the uproar in the Ducal household was, it seems, beyond description. Two detachments of dragoons were at once sent in pursuit of the two carriages which were known to have left the town that night. (How we blessed Anna's shrewder scheme!) When they returned, empty-handed of course, the nature of the trick was perceived. Prince Eugen — whose fury, it appears, was something quite appalling to behold, not only because of the reassertion of the Princess's independence, but because the man whom he had taken so much trouble to obliterate had presumed to be alive after all! — Prince Eugen, according to his wont, took matters into his own hands. He sallied forth with his henchman the doctor, to make inquiries for himself in the town. The result of these was the discovery of the passage of one Hans Meyerhofer's cart out by the South Gate after closing hours. This man was known to the doctor (whose stables he supplied with fodder) as being Anna's cousin, and the connection of the Princess's nurse with the scheme of escape was well demonstrated by her own disappearance. This discovery was sufficient for the Margrave, and (very much, it would appear, against the real wishes of the Duke, whose most earnest desire was to proceed with as little scandal as possible) he with half a dozen troopers instantly set forth in pursuit on the road to Prague. Of these troopers, as we had seen, most had broken down on the way, and none had been able to keep up with the higher mettled mount of their leader — fortunately for us.

It was after his departure that Madam Lothner wrote. She was convinced, as she characteristically remarked, that the Prince would be successful, and that the most dire misfortunes were about to fall upon everybody — all through the obstinacy of M. de Jennico, who really could not say he had not been warned. Nevertheless, on the chance of their having escaped, either to England or to Tollendhal (and she addressed her letter to Tollendhal, trusting that it would be forwarded), she could not refrain from pouring forth her soul into her beloved Princess's bosom — and so forth and so on. In fact, the good woman had wanted a confidant, and had found it on paper.

Our next information regarding the Court of Lausitz came from a very different source, and was of a totally different description. It was the announcement in the Vienna News-Sheet of the death of Eugen, Margrave of Liegnitz-Rothenburg, through a fall from his horse upon a hunting expedition. It was also stated that, yielding at last to her repeated requests, the Duke had consented to the retirement into a convent of his only daughter, Princess Marie Ottilie, such having been (it was stated) her ardent desire for more than a year. The name of the convent was not given.

  *   *   *   *   *   *

Here this memoir, begun in such storm and stress, within and without, continued in such different moods and for such varied motives, ends with the mantle of peace upon us, with the song of birds in our ears.

Tollendhal, that I knew beautiful in the autumn; Tollendhal, the shrine of our young foolish love, is now beautiful with the budding green all round it under a dappled sky. But never had the old stronghouse looked to me so noble as when I brought my bride back to it in the snow. As the carriage at last entered upon the valley road and we saw it rise before us, high against the sky, white-roofed and black-walled, stern, strong, and frowning, while the winter sun flashed back a warm, red welcome to the returning masters, from some high window here and there, I felt my heart stir. And as I looked at Ottilie I saw in her eyes the reflection of the same fire.

Our people had been prepared for our coming by messengers from Prague. The court of honour was thronged, and we entered amid acclamations such as would have satisfied the heart of a king coming to his own again. We had broken the bread and tasted the salt; we had drunk of the wine on the threshold; we had been conducted in state; and at last, at last we found ourselves alone in the old room where my great-uncle's portrait kept its silent watch! János, who, his work of trust done, had fallen back into his place of heiduck as simply as the faithful blade falls back into the scabbard, had retired to his station outside the door. Without rang the wild music of the gipsies to the feasting people, and the tremors of the czimbalom found an answer in the very fibres of my soul — to such music she had first come to me in my dreams!

The walls of the room were all ruddy with the reflection of the bonfire in the courtyard: the very air was filled with joy and colour. And there was my great-uncle's portrait — he was simpering with ineffable complacency; and there the rolled-up parchment; and there the table where we had quarrelled, and where, since then, I had poured forth such mad regrets. Oh! my God! what memories! . . . and there was my wife!

Since the events which had first divided and then reunited us for ever, I had not yet been able to find in the sweet, silent, docile woman I had snatched back to my heart, the wilful Ottilie of old. Her spirits seemed to have been sobered; her gaiety, her petulance, to have been lost in the still current of the almost fearful happiness bought at the price of blood; and at times, in my inmost heart, I had mourned for my lost sprite. But now, as we stood together, she all illumined with the rosy radiance from the fire, she looked of a sudden from the picture on the wall to me, and I saw a spark of the old mockery leap into her eyes.

"And so, sir," she said, "the forward person who married you against your will is mistress here again, after all! . . . but you will always remember, I trust, that it is the privilege of a princess to choose her partner." And then she added, coming a step nearer me: "To-morrow we must fill in the pedigree again — what say you, M. Jean Nigaud de la Faridondaine?"

Now, as she spoke, her lips arched into the well-remembered smile, and beside it danced the dimple. And I know not what came upon me, for there are joys so subtle that they unman even as sorrows, but I fell at her feet with tears.

THE CHOIR INVISIBLE.

By JAMES LANE ALLEN,

Author of "A Summer in Arcady," "A Kentucky Cardinal," etc.

12mo. Cloth. $1.50.

"'The Choir Invisible' bears upon its front that unspeakable repose, that unhurried haste which is the hall-mark of literature; it is alive with the passion of beauty and of pain; it vibrates with that incommunicable thrill which Stevenson called the tuning-fork of art. It is distinguished by a sweet and noble seriousness, through which there strains the sunny light of a glancing humour, a wayward fancy, like sunbeams stealing into a cathedral close through stained-glass windows." — *The Bookman.*

"What impresses one most in this exquisite romance of Kentucky's green wilderness is the author's marvellous power of drawing word-pictures that stand before the mind's eye in all the vividness of actuality. Mr. Allen's descriptions of nature are genuine poetry of form and color." — *The Tribune*, New York.

"The impressions left by the book are lasting ones in every sense of the word, and they are helpful as well. Strong, clear-cut, positive in its treatment, the story will become a power in its way, and the novelist-historian of Kentucky, its cleverest author, will achieve a triumph second to no literary man's in the country." — *Commercial Tribune*, Cincinnati.

"It is this mighty movement of the Anglo-Saxon race in America, this first appearance west of the mountains of civilized white types, that Mr. Allen has chosen as the motive of his historical novel. And in thus recalling 'the immortal dead' he has aptly taken the title from George Eliot's greatest poem. It is by far his most ambitious work in scope, in length, and in character drawing, and in construction. And, while it deals broadly with the beginning of the nation, it gains picturesqueness from the author's *milieu*, as hardly anywhere else were the aristocratic elements of colonial life so contrasted with the rugged life of the backwoods." — *The Journal.*

THE MACMILLAN COMPANY.
66 Fifth Avenue, New York.

Works by F. Marion Crawford.

CORLEONE. By F. Marion Crawford, author of "Saracinesca," "Katharine Lauderdale," "Taquisara," etc. Two volumes in box. $2.00.

"Beginning in Rome, thence shifting to Sicily, and so back and forth, the mere local color of the scene of action is of a depth and variety to excite an ordinary writer to extravagance of diction, to enthusiasm, at least of description; the plot is highly dramatic, not to say sensational. . . .

"Our author has created one of the strongest situations wherewith we are acquainted, either in the novel or the drama.

"Then he has rendered an important service to social science, in addition to creating one of the strongest and most delightful novels of our century."
—*The Bookman.*

A ROSE OF YESTERDAY. Cloth. $1.25.

TAQUISARA. Two volumes. 16mo. In box. $2.00.

CASA BRACCIO. With thirteen full-page illustrations from drawings by Castaigne. Buckram. Two volumes in box. $2.00.

ADAM JOHNSTONE'S SON. With twenty-four full-page illustrations by A. Forestier. 12mo. Cloth. $1.50.

THE RALSTONS. Two volumes. 16mo. Cloth. $2.00.

Uniform Edition of Mr. Crawford's Other Novels.

12mo. Cloth. Price $1.00 each.

Katharine Lauderdale.
Marion Darche.
A Roman Singer.
An American Politician.
Paul Patoff.
Marzio's Crucifix.
Saracinesca.
A Tale of a Lonely Parish.
Zoroaster.
Dr. Claudius.
Mr. Isaacs.
Children of the King.

Pietro Ghisleri.
Don Orsino. A Sequel to "Saracinesca," and "Sant' Ilario."
The Three Fates.
The Witch of Prague.
Khaled.
A Cigarette-Maker's Romance.
Sant' Ilario. A sequel to "Saracinesca."
Greifenstein.
With the Immortals.
To Leeward.

THE MACMILLAN COMPANY,
66 Fifth Avenue, New York.

ALFRED LORD TENNYSON.

A MEMOIR.

BY

HIS SON.

8vo.   Cloth.   Two Vols.   Price, $10.00, *net.*

These volumes of over 500 pages each contain many letters written or received by Lord Tennyson, to which no other biographer could have had access, and in addition a large number of poems hitherto unpublished.

Several chapters are contributed by such of his friends as Dr. Jowett, the Duke of Argyll, the late Earl of Selborne, Mr. Lecky, Professor Francis T. Palgrave, Professor Tyndall, Mr. Aubrey de Vere, and others, who thus express their personal recollections.

There are many illustrations, engraved after pictures by Richard Doyle, Samuel Lawrence, G. F. Watts, R.A., etc., in all about twenty full-page portraits and other illustrations.

COMMENTS.

"The biography is easily the biography not only of the year, but of the decade, and the story of the development of Tennyson's intellect and of his growth — whatever may be the varying opinions of his exact rank among the greatest poets — into one of the few masters of English verse, will be found full of thrilling interest, not only by the critic and student of literature, but by the average reader."
— *The New York Times.*

"Two salient points strike the reader of this memoir. One is that it is uniformly fascinating, so rich in anecdote and marginalia as to hold the attention with the power of a novel. In the next place, it has been put together with consummate tact, if not with academic art. . . .

"It is authoritative if ever a memoir was. But, we repeat, it has suffered no harm from having been composed out of family love and devotion. It is faultless in its dignity." — *The New York Tribune.*

THE MACMILLAN COMPANY,
66 Fifth Avenue, New York.

www.ingramcontent.com/pod-product-compliance
Lightning Source LLC
Chambersburg PA
CBHW032358230426
43672CB00007B/740